SEW MANY BAGS
SEW LITTLE TIME

OVER 30 STYLISH BAGS AND SIMPLE ACCESSORIES

SALLY SOUTHERN

D&C
David and Charles

A DAVID & CHARLES BOOK
Copyright © David & Charles Limited 2008

David & Charles is an F+W Publications Inc. company
4700 East Galbraith Road
Cincinnati, OH 45236

First published in the UK in 2008

Text and designs copyright © Sally Southern 2008
Photography copyright © David & Charles 2008

A catalogue record for this book is available from the British Library.

ISBN-13: 978-0-7153-2649-7 paperback
ISBN-10: 0-7153-2649-X paperback

Printed in China by SNP Leefung Pte Ltd
for David & Charles
Brunel House   Newton Abbot   Devon

Commissioning Editor Jennifer Fox-Proverbs
Desk Editor Bethany Dymond
Senior Designer Charly Bailey
Project Editor Natasha Reed
Production Controller Bev Richardson
Photographers Kim Sayer and Karl Adamson

Visit our website at www.davidandcharles.co.uk

David & Charles books are available from all good bookshops; alternatively you can contact our Orderline on 0870 9908222 or write to us at FREEPOST EX2 110, D&C Direct, Newton Abbot, TQ12 4ZZ (no stamp required UK only); US customers call 800-289-0963 and Canadian customers call 800-840-5220.

Contents

Sew Many Bags …

It's a fact of life that every girl loves bags, and it is never possible to have too many! I'm still putting this theory to the test… This book will give you a taste of how quick and easy (not to mention fun!) it is to make your own bags, choosing fabrics and embellishments that you love!

All the bags featured are simple to make and many of them are suitable for even total beginners who've never picked up a needle and thread in their life. By choosing the fabrics and colours carefully you can have a selection of fantastic bags to cover all occasions, from funky work and shopping bags to cute vanity cases and toiletry bags. And each bag has matching accessories, so you can make purses, notebooks and photo frames too!

You don't need expensive or specialist equipment to make your own bags – just a basic sewing kit and sewing machine. The key to making fabulous bags is to choose the fabrics carefully. Look out for materials that inspire you – they could be bought from haberdashery stores, or from the internet, or you could even use cut-up clothing! Add buttons, beads and sequins, ribbons and braids, or anything else you like!

Bag handles and accessories are becoming ever easier to buy – the internet has a vast selection of suppliers, where you can find all you need. Handles come in a variety of styles and materials, from sophisticated metals and stylish wood to funky coloured plastic, so you can get the look you really want.

This book should inspire you to make bags that suit your own style and personality – and hopefully have fun while doing it!

Happy bag making!

Day Time

Shabby chic

Every girl needs a handbag they can rely on which will hold all your essentials, such as lippy, purse, keys and emergency snacks, but which will also look stylish with whatever you are wearing. This classic tote bag is the simplest bag to make ever. Suitable for even the most unsure beginner, you can make this bag in any fabric, in any colour and in any size to match every outfit!

LOVE THE LOOK?

Follow the same design to create loads of different styles of bag with different materials and textures, for example swirly patterns sewn in, fabric floral embellishments and attention-grabbing materials (see pages 14–21).

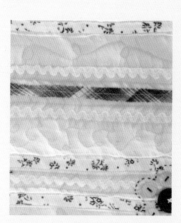
Lace and ribbon

Sweet treat

Simply dotty

Funky florals

fabulous fabric

Choose two contrasting fabrics which work well together. I've chosen a floral cotton fabric with a retro feel, and matched it with a cotton spotted fabric in green. Both the fabrics should be made out of the same fabric (e.g. cotton). They are also paired with a bright yellow cotton as a lining fabric – for linings you can be as bold as you like with colour to really make it stand out when you peek inside the bag!

bag the essentials:

❀ Floral cotton fabric
❀ Green spotted cotton fabric
❀ Yellow cotton fabric
❀ Red gingham ribbon, 1.5cm (⅝in) width
❀ Red gingham ribbon, 0.5cm (²∕₁₀in) width
❀ 2 bamboo 'D' shape handles
❀ Cream machine thread
❀ Basic bag kit (see page 101)

finished size 30 x 23.5cm (12 x 9in)

1 Cut two pieces of floral fabric, each 26 x 24cm (10 x 9²∕₅in), then trim two pieces of green spotted fabric, each 26 x 11cm (10 x 4³∕₁₀in). Cut two pieces of yellow fabric, which will be the lining of the bag, each 33 x 26cm (13 x 10in). Pin the floral fabric to the green spotted fabric along the 26cm (10in) edge, right sides together, and sew. Open the seams and press with an iron.

2 Cut two lengths of red gingham ribbon with a width of 1.5cm (⅝in), each 26cm (10in). Use fabric glue to carefully stick the ribbon along the join of the fabrics and leave to dry completely.

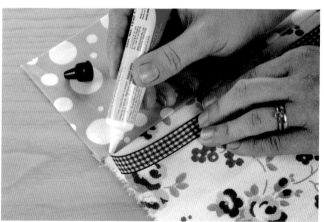

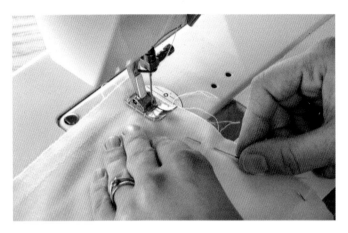

3 When dry, place the front and back panels of the bag together, right sides facing each other and pin along the sides and bottom. Sew these three sides together. Do the same with the lining fabric.

4 Turn the bag through to the right side and press flat. Keep the lining inside out. Push the lining inside the bag and smooth so it fits properly. Fold the top edge of the bag over two times so that it covers the lining and there are no raw edges showing. Press with the iron and pin in place. Sew around the top edge.

5 Cut four lengths of the 0.5cm (⅛in) width red gingham ribbon, each 10cm (4in) long. Carefully thread each length through the hole at the bottom of the bamboo handles.

6 Pin the ribbons that hold the handles in place at the top of the bag, inside the opening and secure with small stitches.

ARM CANDY
Make sure that the two fabrics you choose to use for the outside of the bag match well and are of a similar texture and weight.

Funky florals

This bag is maybe the simplest bag to make – the front and back panels are made from bought place mats, which are the ideal size for this bag. Simply sew them together along three sides, add straps and voila! At last you can have a bag which is big enough to hold all your favourite magazines, so you are never behind on what's happening in the world of celebdom.

1 Take one of the fabric place mats and decorate the front by tracing a leaf pattern (see page 119) onto bondaweb and ironing onto the back of red floral fabric. Cut out and then iron down the right-hand side of the front panel of the bag.

2 Trace two flower shapes (see page 119) onto bondaweb and iron onto the back of plain red fabric. Cut out and iron on top of the leaf shapes. Stitch buttons in the centre of the flowers with red embroidery thread. Place the front and back panels of the bag together and pin along the sides and bottom, then stitch.

3 Use fabric glue to stick a length of red ric rac braid along the top edges of the bag and wait until dry. Pin and stitch red bias binding ribbon along the sides and bottom of the bag.

4 Cut two lengths of pale blue grosgrain ribbon, 1.5cm (⅝in) in width, each 65cm (26in), and stitch inside the top edges of the bag, to make straps.

ARM CANDY
Choose a large print, as the bag is fairly large, and stick to a simple colour scheme – two colours for the background (blue and white) and a bright colour for contrast (in this case, red).

bag the essentials:

❋ 2 fabric place mats, blue and white floral print
❋ Red cotton fabric
❋ Red floral print fabric
❋ Red bias binding
❋ Red ric rac braid
❋ 2 white buttons
❋ Pale blue grosgrain ribbon, 1.5cm (⅝in) wide
❋ Red embroidery thread
❋ Red sewing machine thread
❋ Basic bag kit (see page 101)

finished size 38 x 33.5cm (15 x 13⅛in)

Lace and ribbon

Be the envy of all your friends with a pretty quilted bag. Quilting isn't nearly as tricky as it looks and the results are fantastic! Use buttons to make the simple flower motif on the front and keep colours to a minimum. The fabric used to make this bag already had strips of ribbon stitched onto it but you can achieve the same effect by sewing ribbons onto plain white cotton.

1 Make a paper template for the shape of the bag (see page 117) and cut out two pieces for the front and back, plus two pieces in plain white cotton for the lining. Also cut out two pieces of thin wadding to the same size. Pin all three layers together, with the wadding in between the front fabric and the lining.

2 On a sewing machine, drop the feed dog and sew swirly patterns freehand to give a quilted look. Alternatively you could quilt the fabrics by sewing tiny running stitched swirls. Do this on both the front and back panels. At the bottom right-hand corner of the front panel sew a large red button with six small white buttons around it so that it looks like a flower.

3 Sew small red running stitches around the outside of the buttons to give the flower a more definite shape. Fold the top edges of the front and back panels twice and sew to make a neat hem. Place the front and back pieces together, right sides facing each other, pin along the sides and bottom, and sew.

4 Finish by stitching a handle made of clear plastic beads threaded onto thin wire at either side of the bag.

ARM CANDY
If you can't find handles made from large clear beads like this one, simply buy beads and thread them onto thin jewellery wire to make your own version.

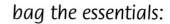

Simply dotty

Bold patterns are the next big thing in bags. Using brightly coloured felt and beads on this neutral coloured bag really gives it a lift. Make sure you also choose a bright contrasting fabric for the lining too.

bag the essentials:

- ❀ Stone coloured spotted cotton fabric
- ❀ Stone floral cotton fabric
- ❀ Hot pink cotton fabric
- ❀ Felt in turquoise, orange, lime and hot pink
- ❀ Felt balls, various sizes, same colours as felt
- ❀ Embroidery thread in hot pink, turquoise and orange
- ❀ Seed beads and sequins, bright colours
- ❀ Cotton woven ribbon, cream
- ❀ Cream sewing machine thread
- ❀ Basic bag kit (see page 101)

finished size 24 x 20cm (9⅕ x 7⁹/₁₀in)

1 Cut two pieces of stone spotted fabric 19 x 22cm (7.5 x 8⁷/₁₀in), and two pieces of stone floral fabric 10 x 22cm (4 x 8⁷/₁₀in). Cut two pieces of bright pink cotton fabric for the lining, 27 x 22cm (10³/₅ x 8⁷/₁₀in). This bag is made up in the same way as the shabby chic tote bag on page 10.

2 Sew large stitches in pink embroidery thread along the join of the two fabrics at the front, and a row of pink running stitch along the top edge of the bag. Use the templates (see page 117) to cut two flowers out of felt, one in turquoise and one in lime green.

3 Sew blanket stitch around the edge of the turquoise flower in orange thread and running stitch along the centre of the lime green petals. Cut out a bright pink circle to go in the centre of the flower (see page 117) and sew running stitch around the edge in turquoise thread. Take a small orange felt ball and sew red seed beads onto it, with a turquoise sequin with a red bead on it at the top. This will go at the centre of the flower.

4 Stitch the finished flower onto the bag. Sew a large pink felt ball with orange seed beads in the top centre. Sew pink running stitch along the centre of a 14cm (5.5in) length of cream cotton woven ribbon. Stitch at the top of the back panel to make a loop to fasten onto the pink ball. Cut a 120cm (47in) length of the same ribbon and sew pink running stitch along the middle. Sew this at the sides to make a long strap. Thread several felt balls together and decorate with seed beads to make a bag charm.

ARM CANDY
When attaching the strap for this bag, make sure it's the right length for you by pinning it first and trying it on before you stitch it in place.

Sweet treat

This delicious-looking handbag looks good enough to eat! To stop this being too 'cutesy' I've used a grey felt to make the bag, and added sweet looking fabric and beads to add decoration. The candy striped handles also add to the fun theme of the bag and lighten the severity of the grey background. As it's made out of felt there's no need for hemming, as felt doesn't fray and is extremely easy to use. The details really make the bag, so spend time choosing beads, buttons and fabrics carefully.

1 Make a paper template (see page 120) for the shape of the bag, with the top edge 21.5cm (8⁵⁄₁₀in) and a depth of 17cm (6.5in). Use the template to cut out two pieces of thick grey felt. Trace the shapes needed for the cupcake (see page 121) onto bondaweb and then iron onto the back of the relevant fabrics (white felt for the icing, beige felt for the cake, pink spotted cotton for the case).

2 Cut out the shapes and position onto the front of one of the grey felt pieces and iron to fix in place. Hand stitch around the edges of the

shapes and to make the stripes on the case. Sew a few multi-coloured seed beads onto the icing and stitch a red button on the top like a cherry.

3 Along the top edge of the bag, sew a row of small white buttons using pink thread. Place a length of ruffled pink and white striped ribbon between the front and back panels of the bag, pin and stitch. Cut four lengths of pale pink ribbon, 1cm (½in) width, and thread through the holes at the bottom of the striped plastic 'D' shaped handles. Stitch the ribbons at the top of the bag to secure the handles in place.

bag the essentials:

- ❀ Grey thick felt
- ❀ Craft felt in beige and white
- ❀ Pink spotted cotton fabric
- ❀ Embroidery thread in pink
- ❀ Seed beads, various colours
- ❀ Red button
- ❀ Several small white buttons
- ❀ Pink and white striped 'D' shaped handles
- ❀ Pale pink ribbon,1cm (½in) width
- ❀ Pink and white striped ruffle ribbon
- ❀ Basic bag kit (see page 101)

finished size 18 x 23cm (7 x 9in)

ARM CANDY
You can afford to go over the top with cuteness on this bag – look out for beads and buttons that look like candies!

Girl about town

This simple bag can be relied upon every day with its sturdy shape, zip fastening and two patch pockets. It's large enough for all your day-to-day needs – diary, phone, purse, make-up – not to mention the massive collection of not-so-essential items we all seem to accumulate! The pockets and embellishment are made from a selection of tweeds in a rich brown and moss-green colour palette.

LOVE THE LOOK?

If you like the look, but want to make something quickly, then try embellishing a diary or notebook cover. It uses the same fabrics and basic stitches to transform a plain book into something special (see page 27).

fabulous fabric

This is quite a wintry looking bag, made out of tweed and wool fabrics in shades of heather purples and mossy greens. The mixture of different patterns and textures within the colour scheme adds interest. You can also make this bag using a lighter colour scheme to give it a more summery feel. To achieve this, stick to heavy cottons and avoid using woollen fabrics.

bag the essentials:

* Tweed-type fabrics in purple, brown and green tones
* 2 large wooden buttons
* 1 medium wooden button
* Sewing machine thread, deep purple
* Embroidery thread in brown, moss green and heather
* Purple zip, 36cm (14³⁄₁₆in)
* Safety pin
* Basic bag kit (see page 101)

finished size 60 x 40cm (24 x 16in)

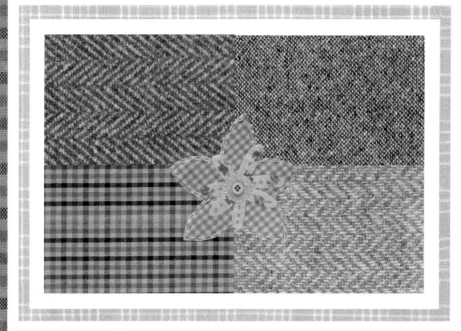

1 Cut two pieces of purple tweed fabric 28 x 38cm (11 x 15in). This will form the front and back of the bag. Cut another piece 10 x 90cm (4 x 36in) for the strap. Choose two brown fabrics and cut out of each a piece measuring 12 x 15.5cm (4³⁄₄ x 6¹⁄₈in) for the pockets. Put these pieces to one side.

2 Use the patterns provided on page 118 to trace a large flower, a small flower and a circle onto bondaweb. Roughly cut out the shapes and iron onto the back of the fabrics you have chosen. Cut out.

3 Position the large flower at the bottom left hand corner of one of the purple pieces of tweed. Peel off the backing and iron to fix in place. Place the smaller flower onto the large flower and the circle in the centre and iron in place. Use the green thread to sew around the edge of the large flower twice in running stitch; the purple thread to over-stitch around the edge of the smaller flower and to sew a running stitch border around it; and the brown thread to stitch the circle in place and sew small stitches along the centre of the small flower petals. In the middle of the circle sew a medium-sized wooden button.

4 Trace two shapes from the patterns provided onto bondaweb for the tops of the pockets. Choose two fabrics and iron these shapes onto the back, then cut out. Take the two pieces of brown fabric cut to be pockets and place the shapes you've just cut at the top. Peel off the paper backing and iron to fix in place. Sew around the bottom edge of these shapes in running stitch. Sew a large wooden button onto each pocket.

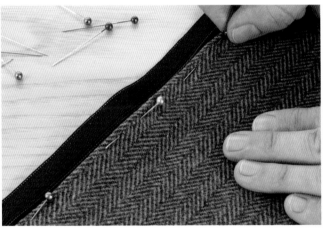

5 Fold the edges of the pockets under by 1cm (⅜in) at the sides and bottom, and 2cm (¾in) at the top, then press with an iron. Hem the top edge with machine stitches. Pin the pockets in position on the front panel of the bag and machine stitch around the three sides, leaving the top of the pockets open. Stitch along the sides and bottom of the pockets with green thread, and then along the top with purple thread.

6 Take the front panel of the bag, turn under the top edge by 1cm (⅜in) and press. Pin one side of the zip in position and sew in place. Repeat with the back panel.

ARM CANDY
As an alternative to wooden buttons, use oversized shiny buttons in plastic or metal. They'll still complement the design, but will catch the light and glint against the darker background.

7 Turn the fabric right sides together and pin around the remaining three sides of the bag. Machine stitch around the edges, leaving a 1cm (⅜in) hem. Turn the bag through to the right side and press with the iron.

8 Take the length of fabric cut for the strap and fold in half long ways, right sides together. Pin the raw edges together along the length and then machine stitch. Turn the strap through to the right side, using a safety pin to pull it through. Press flat with the iron, then machine stitch down each side of the strap, 5mm (³⁄₁₆in) from the edge.

9 Fold under the raw ends of the strap and pin the strap onto the back of the bag, 4cm (1½in) from the top edge. Stitch the strap in place by sewing a square with a cross in the middle to make it more secure.

LIGHTEN UP

For a lighter, brighter look, make the bag using a selection of cotton fabrics in faded denim style blues. Mix small checks and sweet florals for a vintage patchwork effect that gives the design a real homespun feel.

I'll check my diary

Make sure you never miss a hot date or important appointment with this nifty notebook, made to match the satchel.

bag the essentials:

❁ Plain covered notebook, A6 size (4³⁄₁₆ x 5¹⁄₂in)
❁ Selection of tweed and check fabrics
❁ 20cm (8in) purple ribbon, 5mm (³⁄₁₆in) wide
❁ 2 small beige buttons
❁ Embroidery threads in green and brown
❁ Basic bag kit (see page 101)

finished size 15 x 11cm (6 x 4³⁄₁₀in)

1 Cut a piece of green tweed 7 x 20cm (2¾ x 8in). Fold under the long edges by 1cm (⅜in), press with an iron and pin. Sew running stitch in brown thread along the edges.

2 Stick this panel onto the front of the book 2cm (¾in) in from the opening edge using double-sided tape. Use fabric glue to stick the purple ribbon onto the panel along the right hand edge; fold the edges of the panel over inside the book.

3 Trace the patterns for the two flowers (see page 118) onto bondaweb, and roughly cut out each piece. Iron onto the back of your chosen fabrics and cut out. Peel the backing from the inner flowers and the centre circle and iron to fix in place.

4 Sew around the edge of the flowers with green thread. With brown thread sew over-stitch around the circle and sew purple stitches along the petals of the inner flowers. Sew a small button in the centre of each. Stick double-sided tape onto the back of the two flowers and adhere onto the front of the book, folding any petals that go over the edge inside the cover.

5 Finish by sticking the first page of the book onto the inside cover to hide the raw edges and give a neat finish.

Nature girl

Make a handy big bag that's also super-stylish too! It's just the right size to carry magazines, books, folders and all those 'must-have' accessories to see you through the day. Throw in a matching mp3 player case and mobile or cell phone pouch and you're good to go! Try to use sturdy fabrics, such as furnishing fabrics which come in fantastic and funky designs to make your bag practical as well as looking good!

LOVE THE LOOK?

A stylish pouch can also be made using a matching piece of fabric from the bag. Ideal as an mp3 player case, mobile phone pouch or sunglasses holder! See page 33 for details.

fabulous fabric

For this bag I chose a large print heavy cotton furnishing fabric to make the body of the bag in green, cream and browns. To contrast with this I found a plain green fabric in the same weight. As it's a large bag, look for fabric with a large scale print.

bag the essentials:

❋ Furnishing fabric in beige leaf and flower print
❋ Lime green furnishing fabric
❋ Beige lining material
❋ Strengthening Vilene
❋ Magnetic fastening snaps
❋ 4 metal stud feet
❋ Bag bottom stiffener
❋ Safety pin
❋ Basic bag kit (see page 101)

finished size 28 x 40cm (11 x 16in)

1 Cut the printed fabric so that you have a piece 30 x 37cm (12 x 14½ in) and a piece 58 x 37cm (22⅘ x 14⅗in). Trim the stiffener so that you have two pieces the same size as the printed fabric pieces. Cut the lime green fabric so that you have a piece 95 x 12cm (37⅖ x 4⁷⁄₁₀in). Tack the stiffener onto the back of the printed fabrics.

2 The smaller piece of printed fabric will be the front of the bag, the larger piece will be the back panel and front flap. Pin the long green strip of fabric so that it goes down one side of the patterned fabric, along the bottom and up the other side (right sides together). Sew, and then pin and sew the back panel in place too. Turn through to the right side so you have a bag shape. Now remove the tacking stitches.

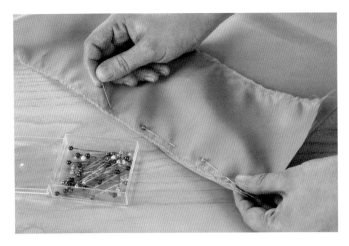

3 Cut the lining fabric so that you have a piece 37 x 100cm (14³⁄₅ x 39²⁄₅in), and two pieces 30 x 12cm (12 x 4⁷⁄₁₀in). Pin the smaller panels down the long edges of the lining material, along the bottom of the small panels and up the other edge at each side, so that you have a bag shape similar to the one you've just made. Sew the lining pieces together.

4 Turn the main bag inside out again, and slide the lining fabric over it. Pin and sew, leaving the edge at the end of the front flap open. Turn the bag through to the right side so that the lining is in place.

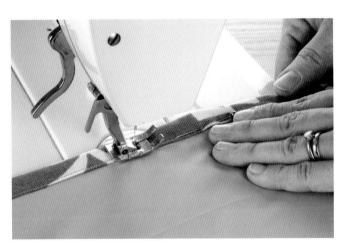

5 Double fold the open edge at the front flap inwards, pin and stitch to make a neat hem.

6 Cut a piece of bag bottom stiffener 35 x 10cm (13½ x 4in) and cover it with the patterned fabric, using double-sided tape.

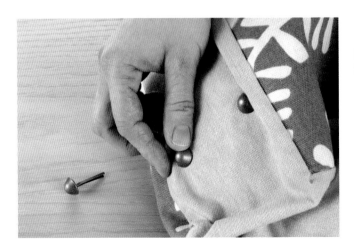

7 Place the covered panel at the bottom of the bag and secure in place by attaching the metal stud feet to the bottom of the bag and through the stiffener board.

8 Mark the position of the magnetic snap fastener on the front of the bag and the inside of the flap, and then attach them in place.

9 Cut out a circle of patterned fabric backed with bondaweb (to prevent fraying) that will cover the magnetic snap on the front of the flap and then stitch it in place.

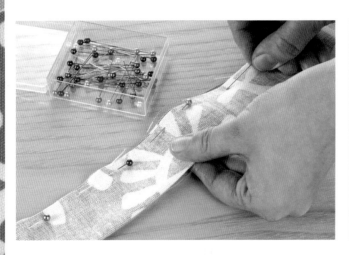

10 Cut a length of patterned fabric 8 x 122cm (3 x 47¾in) to form the strap. Fold in half along the length, right sides together, pin and sew.

11 Use a safety pin to turn the strap through to the right side. Press with an iron, and then sew again along either side 0.5cm (½in) in from each edge.

12 Fold the raw edges of the strap under and pin onto each side of the bag. Stitch securely in place.

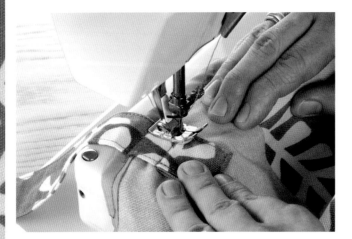

ARM CANDY
This bag is ideal for college or work – you could stitch a couple of simple pockets into the lining to keep smaller items such as your phone, pens and mp3 player.

Just in case

If you've ever rummaged around in the bottom of your bag for your phone, sunglasses or mp3 player you will be glad of this handy little item to keep everything in its rightful place.

ARM CANDY
Make this pouch in the same way, but alter the sizes to make a snazzy sunglasses case.

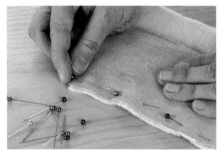

1 Cut a piece of cream fleece 12 x 14cm (4⁷⁄₁₀ x 5.5in), and a piece of green fabric 8 x 14cm (3 x 5.5in). Pin the two fabrics together along the 14cm (5.5in) edge and sew.

3 Fold the panel of fabric in half, right sides together, and pin along the side and bottom, leaving the top open. Sew. Open seam and press.

2 Back patterned fabric with bondaweb and cut out a flower. Put in centre of cream fleece, iron and sew round edge. Fold over green fabric, leaving a 4cm (1.5in) border above cream fabric. Pin and sew 1cm (½in) above join of fleece and green fabric.

4 Turn through to the right side, and press flat. Cut thin cream ribbon 10cm (4in) long. Fold in half and sew the raw edges in the middle top on the back of the pouch so that you have a fastening loop. Sew a green wooden bead onto the front to fasten.

bag the essentials:

❁ Cream fleece fabric
❁ Lime green furnishing fabric
❁ Patterned furnishing fabric
❁ Green wooden bead
❁ Cream ribbon, 0.3cm (²⁄₁₀in) width
❁ Basic bag kit (see page 101)

finished size 13 x 6cm (5 x 2.5in)

Moody blues

Now you don't have to throw away your favourite pair of jeans when they finally fall to bits – you can recycle them by making this cool backpack and giving them a second chance to look stylish! Use the details of the jeans as funky features in the bag – frayed hems and seams as part of the bag itself. Accessorise with your most fitted pair of jeans and you are ready to hit the town.

LOVE THE LOOK?

Use the floral print fabric to make a matching bag charm, luggage label and keyring too (see pages 38–39), any of which would look fabulous attached to the backpack.

fabulous fabric

I love using denim, and I love the fact that this bag is made from old jeans. There are so many great details on jeans that can be incorporated into the design of the bag. As with bought fabrics, you still need to consider the colour of your denim, and ensure that the shades of the various pairs of jeans you use tone together well.

bag the essentials:

❀ Denim jeans, 2 pairs (slightly different shades of denim)
❀ Pale blue gingham fabric
❀ Large floral print cotton fabric
❀ Cream cord
❀ Pale blue grosgrain ribbon, 3cm (1⅕in) width
❀ Safety pin
❀ Basic bag kit (see page 101)

finished size 54 x 37cm (21 x 14⅗in)

1 Cut the legs off the jeans and then cut up one of the seams so that you have large pieces of fabric. Cut two pieces of denim, each 40 x 46cm (16 x 17½in). Use the other pair of jeans to cut another two pieces, each 40 x 14cm (16 x 5½in), if possible using the bottom hem as a 40cm (16in) edge. Pin the large pieces of denim to the smaller ones along the 40cm (16in) edge and stitch together so you have a front and back panel for your bag.

2 Carefully unpick a pocket from the back of one of the pair of jeans to go onto the front of the bag. Try to use a different shade of denim from the main colour of the front of the bag so that it will stand out.

3 Iron bondaweb onto the back of the floral fabric and cut out two large flowers. Position these onto the front panel of the bag and place the pocket on top so that the flowers are slightly behind the pocket, one at the top, one at the bottom at the opposite side. When you're happy with the positioning, lift the pocket and iron the flowers to fix in place. Then pin the pocket in place and sew, leaving the top edge open.

4 Cut the waistbands from the top of the jeans. These will form the straps for the bag. You can fasten the button so that it becomes a feature of the strap. You'll need two straps, about 70cm (27½in) in length.

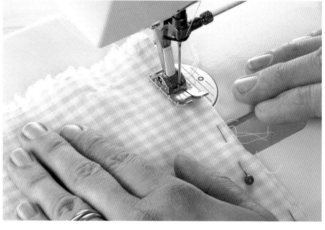

5 Place the front and back panels of the bag right sides together and pin down the sides and along the bottom. Push the straps down into the bag and pin at the bottom corners so that when sewn the straps will be attached at the bottom. Sew along the sides and bottom and then turn through to the right side. Press flat.

6 Make the lining by cutting one piece of pale blue gingham measuring 75 x 60cm (27½ x 24in). Fold in half along the 75cm (27½in) edge, then pin and sew along the side and bottom.

ARM CANDY
You will need to use a special strong needle such as a leather needle for your sewing machine.

7 Push the lining inside the bag. Fold the gingham over twice at the top so that it covers the raw denim edge and pin in place. Pin the straps at the top beneath the gingham border so that they will be secure when stitched. Sew along the top edge of the bag.

8 Pin the blue grosgrain ribbon around the top of the bag 6cm (2½in) down from the top edge, starting at the middle of the front of the bag and folding under the raw edges of the ribbon. Leave a 4cm (1½in) gap between the ends of the ribbon. This will form the drawstring channel so that the bag can be fastened. Sew the ribbon in place at the top and bottom edge. Cut the cream cord 150cm (59in) in length and use a safety pin to thread it through the drawstring channel.

SIMPLY CHARMING

Fashion a cute bag charm to adorn a handbag. Just sandwich a folded length of blue ribbon between two circles of denim, joined with bondaweb. Scratch the raw edges to get a frayed look. Iron on two flowers from fabric and sew around the edge of the denim circle with running stitch in red thread.

FLOWER CHAIN

A matching keyring completes the denim backpack nicely. Sew together the edges of a large flower from the floral fabric and a piece of thin denim the same size. Leave a gap and stuff with a little wadding. Add a folded length of thin red ribbon into the gap of the padded flower and sew up the hole so that the ribbon is secured. Sew around the edge with small stitches in red thread. Thread several wooden beads onto the ribbon and attach a key ring finding at the top.

Romantic break

Make sure your luggage is never misplaced
with this attractive label. You may have to make
several when others spot it!

bag the essentials:

❀ Thin denim fabric
❀ Floral print cotton fabric
❀ Acetate sheet
❀ White card
❀ Red embroidery thread
❀ Red and white striped
  ribbon, 1cm (½in) width
❀ Basic bag kit
  (see page 101)

finished size 10.5 x 5.5cm
(4⅕ x 2⅕in)

ARM CANDY
Sometimes denim from jeans can
be a bit too thick to work with on
smaller items. You might find it
easier to use a denim chambray,
which is a much thinner denim.

1 Cut out two pieces of denim,
12 x 8cm (4⁷⁄₁₀ x 3in). On one mark
the centre aperture, 7 x 3.5cm (2¾ x
1⅖in). Cut a cross in the centre of the
aperture from corner to corner and
trim so that the edges can be folded
under, leaving a neat aperture.

2 Machine stitch around the
aperture, and then sew again in
running stitch with red thread. Fold
under one of the short edges on each
piece of denim and hem. Place the
two bits of denim right sides together
and sew along three edges, leaving
the hemmed edge open. Turn through
to the right side and press. Slide in a
piece of acetate cut to the size of the
luggage label. Iron bondaweb onto
the back of the floral fabric and cut
out two small flowers.

3 Iron the flowers onto the front of
the luggage label so that they
overlap the acetate slightly. (Cover
the acetate with thin fabric when
you iron the flowers in place to avoid
it melting.) Cut a length of red and
white striped ribbon 1cm (½in) wide,
26cm (10in). Fold this in half to make
a loop and sew it into the inside of the
luggage label. Cut a piece of white
card to write your name and address
on and slide this into the luggage
label under the acetate.

Play Time

Sunny afternoon

Whether it's a day at the seaside or a picnic in the park, the cotton fabrics in bright ice-cream colours make this slouchy beach bag the perfect companion. It's spacious enough to hold all the essentials for your lazy day, including your towel, sunglasses, sun cream and even that indulgent blockbuster novel! Trimmed with cute ribbon and simple stitching, the result is as sweet and refreshing as a cool ice cream on a hot day.

LOVE THE LOOK?

Use the same techniques to make this matching girlie picture frame to display your favourite beach holiday photo – guaranteed to make any bedroom feel sunny (see page 48).

fabulous fabric

Choose bright pastel colours in cotton fabrics, and mix contrasting patterns – gingham, spotted and floral. It is essential that you check the fabrics look good together before you start.

bag the essentials:

❁ Pink gingham fabric

❁ Four co-ordinating cotton fabrics in a mix of spots and florals

❁ Six lengths of ribbon in different colours, widths and textures

❁ White cotton fabric (for the butterfly wings)

❁ Pink/peach cotton fabric (for the butterfly bodies)

❁ Three small co-ordinating flower embellishments

❁ Plain pink cotton fabric (for the lining)

❁ Embroidery threads in red, pink, pale pink and green

❁ Machine thread, pink

❁ Basic bag kit (see page 101)

finished size 75 x 50cm (30 x 20in)

1 Make a template for the bag, using the pattern provided on page 125. Pin the template onto the gingham fabric and cut two pieces, allowing an extra 1cm (³⁄₈in) all the way round for seams.

2 Trace the shapes of the patches from the pattern provided onto bondaweb, and iron onto the back of the selected co-ordinating fabrics. Cut out, peel off the paper backing and arrange onto the front of one of the gingham bag shapes. Iron to fix in place.

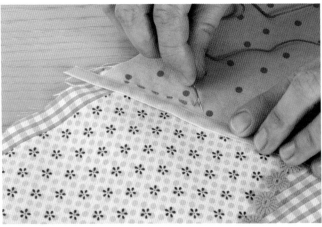

3 Choose where you want each type of ribbon to lie, then cut them to the right lengths, laying them onto the bag. Once you're satisfied with the layout, use fabric glue to stick the ribbons in place. Allow to dry.

4 Add stitching along the edges of the different fabrics and ribbons in a mixture of running stitch and over stitch, using co-ordinating embroidery threads.

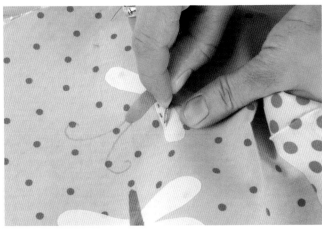

5 Trace the butterfly shapes from the pattern provided on page 125 onto bondaweb and iron the wings onto white cotton fabric and the bodies onto the pink/peach fabric. Cut out and arrange on the front of the bag and iron to fix in place.

6 Sew around the wings in running stitch and sew stripes over the body.

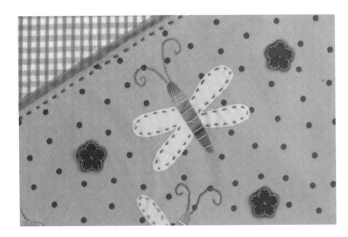

7 Draw antennae onto the butterflies with a fabric marker, then sew over this in back stitch. Use fabric glue to stick three small flower motifs around the butterflies.

ARM CANDY
If you can't resist a little sparkle, use metallic threads to embellish the butterflies and watch them shimmer in the sunlight.

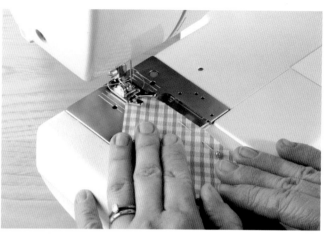

8 Make a template for the lining of the bag (see page 125) and pin onto the plain pink cotton fabric. Cut two pieces, allowing an extra 1cm (³⁄₈in) all the way round for seams.

9 Pin front and the back of the bag together, right sides together, and sew around the edges, leaving a gap where shown on the template for the opening of the bag.

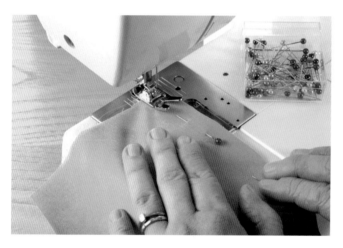

10 Turn the bag through to the right side, pushing through the straps. Press flat with an iron.

11 Pin the front and back of the lining together and sew in the same way as described in step 9.

ARM CANDY
Blue/turquoise is a great complementary colour against the strawberry ice cream shades of this design – it really 'pops'. Use sparingly for the best effect.

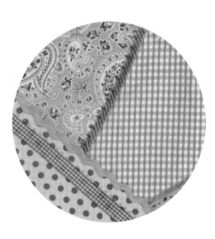

12 Fold the raw edges at the opening of the bag inside and press with an iron, then pin. Do the same with the lining, but fold the raw edges outside. Place the lining inside the bag and pin together along the opening, so that no raw edges can be seen. Then cut two lengths of ribbon, each 20cm (8in), and pin these either side of the opening of the bag in the centre in between the lining and the outside of the bag. Sew the lining and the outside of the bag together.

13 Tie the top of the bag together in a secure knot to complete the strap.

SAFE AND SECURE

Once you've filled you bag, before setting off out for the day, tie a small but secure bow using the two lengths of ribbon you attached in step 12.

Pretty as a picture

This cute picture frame is ideal for using up scraps of fabric and ribbon left over from the bag. It's simply a cardboard template that has been embellished, then secured to your chosen frame.

bag the essentials:

❁ Picture frame, 12.5 x 17.5cm (4⁷/₈ x 6⁷/₈in)
❁ Thick card
❁ Scraps of fabric and ribbon from the bag
❁ Embroidery threads in red, pale green and turquoise green
❁ Large flower motif
❁ Basic bag kit (see page 101)

finished size 12.5 x 17.5cm (4⁹/₁₀ x 6⁹/₁₀in)

1 Make a template for the cardboard frame, working to 12.5 x 17.5cm (4⁷/₈ x 6⁷/₈in). Cut a piece of pink gingham fabric 2cm (³/₄in) bigger than the frame all the way around. Use a fabric marker pen to mark out the window onto the wrong side of the fabric.

ARM CANDY
Use all the yummy scraps of fabrics and ribbons left over from the bag and add bought embellishments for maximum cuteness. The picture frame also makes a great and quick-to-make present!

2 Use the template to trace the shapes you need for the fabric patches and butterfly onto bondaweb. Iron these onto the back of the fabrics and cut out. Position the patches and butterfly onto the gingham fabric and iron to fix in place. Use fabric glue to stick the ribbons in place and allow to dry. Embellish the fabric with stitches, and glue the flower motif to the corner.

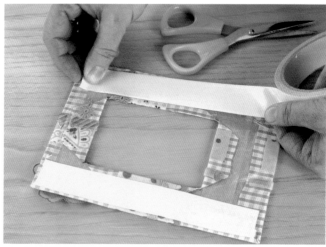

3 Stick double-sided tape onto the front of the cardboard. Position it tape side down above the wrong side of the fabric and stick in place. Use sharp scissors to pierce the centre of the fabric in the window, and cut diagonally to each corner. Stick double-sided tape onto the back of the cardboard and fold the raw edges from the centre of the frame over onto the back so it looks neat from the front. Stick more double-sided tape onto the back of the completed cardboard and then stick it onto the actual picture frame.

Bon voyage

This cute vintage-style case is just the right size to take away on a romantic weekend with a partner. Or if you love it too much to take out of the house, it is perfect to use as a special keepsake box, or to store all your favourite little knick-knacks. You can use it as a gorgeous vanity case and fill it with your favourite cosmetics – with a case this size you may even have an excuse to buy some more!

LOVE THE LOOK?

Use the same methods to fashion an adorable photo album and cute matching greetings card as a special finishing touch. See pages 54 and 55.

fabulous fabric

In contrast to the sunny afternoon bag which mixes lots of colours together to make up its patchwork effect, in this project stick to a colour scheme made up of three fabrics in different prints. I've used pale blue and white as the main colours, and a bit of extra colour is included in the floral patches. The case has a vintage look, using muted pastel shades. If you can't find the fabrics you want, you could try tea staining existing fabrics to give them an aged look.

bag the essentials:

* Small cardboard case
* Cotton fabrics: 3 in shades of blue (spotted, striped, floral); 1 pale green spotted; scraps in 5 different colours and patterns
* Embroidery threads in pale pink, pale blue and pale green
* Pale blue grosgrain ribbon, 2cm (¾in) wide
* Pale blue ribbon, 3cm (1⅕in) wide
* 4 metal stud feet
* Vanishing pen
* Spray adhesive
* Basic bag kit (see page 101)

finished size 35 x 22.5cm (13½ x 8⁹⁄₁₀in)

1 Open the case, lay it onto paper and draw around it to make a paper template.

2 Once you have the size of the case drawn out, you can split it up into patches and allocate the blue fabrics to the patches.

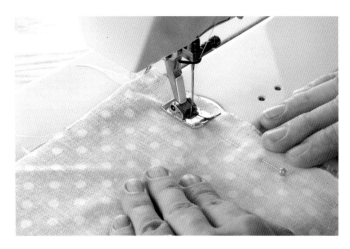

3 Use the template to cut the fabrics to the size needed, remembering to leave a 1cm (½in) edge for sewing together. Pin the pieces together and stitch so you have all the blue cotton fabrics patchworked together.

4 Use the templates (see page 121) to trace the shapes needed for the birds onto bondaweb. Each bird will need a body, a wing and a beak. Iron the bondaweb shapes onto the back of the scraps of fabric and cut out.

5 Arrange these pieces onto the patchwork panel and iron to fix in place. Sew around the birds with catch stitches in embroidery thread. Sew around the wing and beak in running stitch, and add a french knot for the eye. Draw three swirls as tail feathers at the back of each bird, then sew running stitch along the lines. Weave a contrasting coloured thread between the running stitch. When the birds are embroidered, sew along the joins of the patchwork with embroidery thread, using a variety of large stitches.

6 Make a paper template that will fit around the handle and clasp at the front of the case and then use this to cut the green spotted fabric to size. Use spray adhesive, sprayed lightly onto the back of this fabric panel, to stick it in place. Cut two long strips of green spotted fabric to go along the sides of the case, and fold under the raw edges. Stitch these edges with running stitch in blue thread and stick these panels in place with double-sided tape.

ARM CANDY
You can change the colour scheme to suit your taste – instead of making it in blues and whites, why not try using brighter colours and bolder prints? You can use the same technique to cover box files too, for smaller keep-sake boxes.

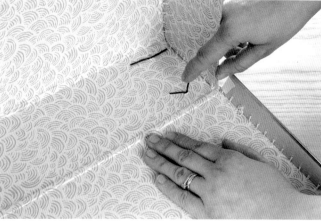

7 Stick the patchwork panel onto the main body of the case, using double-sided tape. Cover all the raw edges with ribbon, sticking it on with double-sided tape. Use the grosgrain ribbon for the top and bottom edges of the case, and the wider ribbon at the edge that gets covered when the lid is closed. Fold under and then secure the raw edges to neaten.

8 Make four small holes on the base of the case, push the metal studs through and secure inside.

SPECIAL GREETINGS

The photo album and weekend case would make a fabulous gift for a loved one – why not make this matching card too. Take a small white card with an aperture and cut a piece of blue spotted fabric larger than the aperture. Trace the bird shapes onto bondaweb and iron the shapes onto the relevant bits of fabric. Cut out and arrange onto the blue fabric panel. Iron and decorate with stitching. Take the card blank and stitch small blue stitches around the aperture onto the card. Stick the finished panel into the card using double-sided tape.

Magic memories

Remember all your favourite times with an attractive photo album, using the same fabrics and pattern as the vanity case.

bag the essentials:

❋ Same selection of fabrics as described for the case
❋ Small photo album
❋ Pale blue polka dot print paper
❋ Basic bag kit (see page 101)

finished size 18 x 12cm (7 x 4⁷⁄₁₀in)

ARM CANDY
Instead of using fabrics to cover the album, why not try using pretty craft or wrapping paper?

1 Make a paper template for the cover of the photo album, and split it up into patches. Cut one piece of blue print fabric large enough to cover the whole photo album and use squares of the matching fabrics backed with bondaweb to make the patchwork effect. Arrange these patches onto the main base fabric and iron to fix in place. Make the bird motif (see page 121 for the templates) as described for the vanity case and decorate with stitches in the same way. Stitch along the edges of the patches with a variety of stitches.

2 When the fabric panel is finished, use it to back the photo album using double-sided tape. Cut two panels of polka dot print paper to stick inside the front and back covers to cover the raw edges of fabric. Stick these paper pieces in place with double-sided tape.

Shopaholic!

This value-for-money bag is reversible so you get two looks in one (see page 61). Ideal for those days when you can't find the exact bag to go with your perfect outfit, now you can simply turn the bag inside out to get a completely fresh look. It's also really spacious with a wide opening so you can really go to town with your shopping too! The corsage is removable, and you can even make a themed purse to go with it.

LOVE THE LOOK?

No bag is complete without an adorable purse too. Continue the floral theme with a matching purse made out of felt. So cute everyone will want one! See page 63 for details.

fabulous fabric

Choose bold colours for this bag, in cotton fabrics. The simple palette of red, white and blue works really well. The floral and polka dot prints contrast fantastically, but because only three colours are used, everything matches harmoniously.

1 Cut two pieces of the white and blue print fabric, 40 x 52cm (16 x 20½in), and two pieces of the red polka dot fabric the same size. Trace one large and two small flower shapes and centres (see page 124) onto bondaweb and iron onto the reverse of the various red fabrics. Cut out the shapes and arrange them at the bottom right hand corner of one of the pieces of white and blue print fabric.

2 Mark each of the pieces of fabric at either side, 18cm (7in) from the top. Place the two pieces of white and blue print fabrics together, right sides facing and pin and sew down the sides and along the bottom from the mark at one side to the mark at the other. Repeat this process with the red polka dot fabrics.

bag the essentials:

❁ White cotton fabric with blue floral print
❁ Red polka dot cotton fabric
❁ Plain red cotton fabric
❁ White and red polka dot cotton fabric
❁ Navy felt
❁ Selection of red and blue ribbons and ric rac braid
❁ 2 hoop handles
❁ Small red button
❁ Safety pin
❁ Basic bag kit (see page 101)

finished size 50 x 34cm (19½ x 13⅖in)

3 Turn one of the bags through to the right side and place one bag inside the other. Fold in and press the sides of the bags that haven't been sewn and stitch them up so that the two bags are now stitched together along this seam.

4 Cut two pieces of plain red fabric each 42 x 12cm (16½ x 4⁷⁄₁₀in). On each piece, fold under and press along each long edge so that the raw edge is hidden and then fold under the ends by 1cm (½in) and press, pin and then sew.

5 Fold the red fabric pieces in half long ways and pin and sew along the top edge of the front opening of the bag. Now repeat with the top edge of the back opening of the bag.

6 Take one of the handles, fold the red fabric over it, pin and sew so that the handle is attached. Repeat with the other handle.

7 Hand stitch small stitches at either end of the red fabric close to the handle.

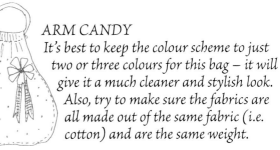

ARM CANDY
It's best to keep the colour scheme to just two or three colours for this bag – it will give it a much cleaner and stylish look. Also, try to make sure the fabrics are all made out of the same fabric (i.e. cotton) and are the same weight.

Pretty petals

Change your look again with this funky detachable corsage.
Featuring colours and fabrics from both sides of the bag
ensures that it will go perfectly with either side, creating
several fab looks with just a few minor adjustments.

To make the corsage

1 Make the corsage by cutting a large flower out of navy
felt and stitching small red running stitch around the
edges. Iron bondaweb onto the back of the white and blue
floral fabric and cut out a flower shape from flower print
fabric. Iron at the centre of the felt flower, and sew a small
red button in the middle.

2 Cut several strands of red and blue ribbons to various
lengths and stitch at the back of the corsage. Sew a
safety pin onto the back of the corsage so that it can be
pinned onto the bag.

ARM CANDY
*This corsage is detachable so that you
can use it on both sides of the bag, or
remove it and wear it as a brooch.*

DOUBLE TROUBLE

*Simply turn the bag
inside out to reveal
a completely new
theme from the
floral side. Add the
dainty corsage and
get ready paint
the town red!*

Money bags

Be the envy of all your friends and acquaintances with a sweet little purse for keeping all your spare change in. When buying the metal clasp fastening for the purse, try to get one that can be stitched onto, instead of glued. This makes it much easier to attach the felt body of the purse, especially as felt doesn't fray and doesn't need hemming.

bag the essentials:

❀ Felt, navy blue and red
❀ Purse fastening
❀ Navy blue embroidery thread
❀ White and navy print fabric
❀ Small red button
❀ Basic bag kit (see page 101)

finished size 9.5 x 8cm (3⁷⁄₁₀ x 3in)

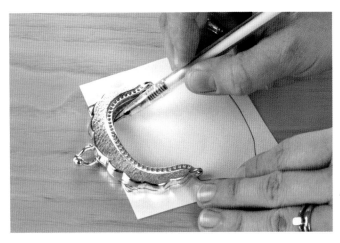

1 Draw around your purse fastening and make a paper template for the purse.

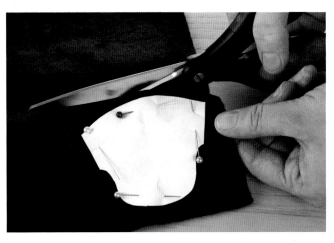

2 Cut out two pieces in navy felt.

3 Cut out a red felt flower and bondaweb a blue print flower in the centre. Sew around the edge of the flower with blue running stitch. Sew a small red button in the centre of the flower, attaching the flower to one of the pieces of blue felt.

4 Place the two pieces of navy blue felt together, right sides facing and sew around the edges from the two points where the frame will attach. Turn through to the right side and press. Stitch the purse onto the frame, front and back.

Glitz & glamour

This is a real cutie of a bag, and very simple to make too! Just the right size to fit your phone, purse and lip-gloss. Felt is so easy to work with as it doesn't fray, so there's no need to hem the edges. Use thicker felt than normal craft felt for a much sturdier shape to your bag – Nepal wool felt is ideal as it has greater thickness and a texture than regular felt, but still feels soft.

LOVE THE LOOK?

Accessorise your evening bag with a sophisticated necklace (see page 67), which will look wonderful with your little black dress. Using the same crochet lace as the bag, black and cream is the hippest colour combination to be seen in this season.

fabulous fabric

It's really worth trying to find a heavy weight felt to make this bag instead of the normal felt. This will make sure that the bag will hold its shape well and not be too floppy. This bag is made out of thick black felt, which is much denser than craft felt.

bag the essentials:

❋ Thick black felt
❋ Cream cotton crochet lace
❋ Woollen crochet brooch
❋ Flat pearl beads
❋ Black seed beads
❋ Black thread
❋ Basic bag kit (see page 101)

finished size 30 x 26cm (12 x 10in)

1 Make a paper template of the size of the bag (see page 116). Pin this onto the felt and mark around the template with a fabric pencil. Cut out two pieces of felt, including the centre piece that forms the handle so you have a front and back panel.

2 Pin cream lace around the outer edge of one of the felt pieces, and then sew in place.

3 Lay the front and back panels together and pin at the sides, at the point where you want the opening to be. Mark this point with fabric pencil at each side.

4 Now pin and sew the lace onto the front piece of the bag, from one marked point to the other, along the top edge, as shown.

EVENING DRESS

Accessorise your beautiful bag with a matching necklace. Cut a length of black cotton crochet lace 40cm (16in) long, or as long as you require the necklace to be. At each end, stitch a tiny piece of black felt to cover the raw edges. Cut a flower shape out of black felt (see page 117) and stitch this onto the lace, slightly off centre from the middle point. Sew three small cream flower shaped buttons in the centre of the flower, using black embroidery thread. Finish by stitching a metal ring and clasp fastening at the ends of the lace.

5 Pin the corsage in place on the front panel of the bag and then mark with fabric pencil the places where you want the beads to be stitched. Sew the beads in place, with a black seed bead on top of a flat pearl bead. Pin the front and back pieces of the bag together, remembering to leave the opening at the top.

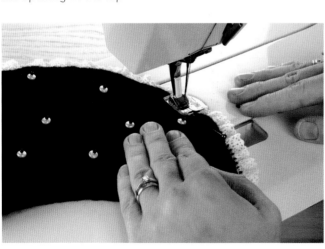

6 Now sew the bag together, from one marked point to the other.

Home Time

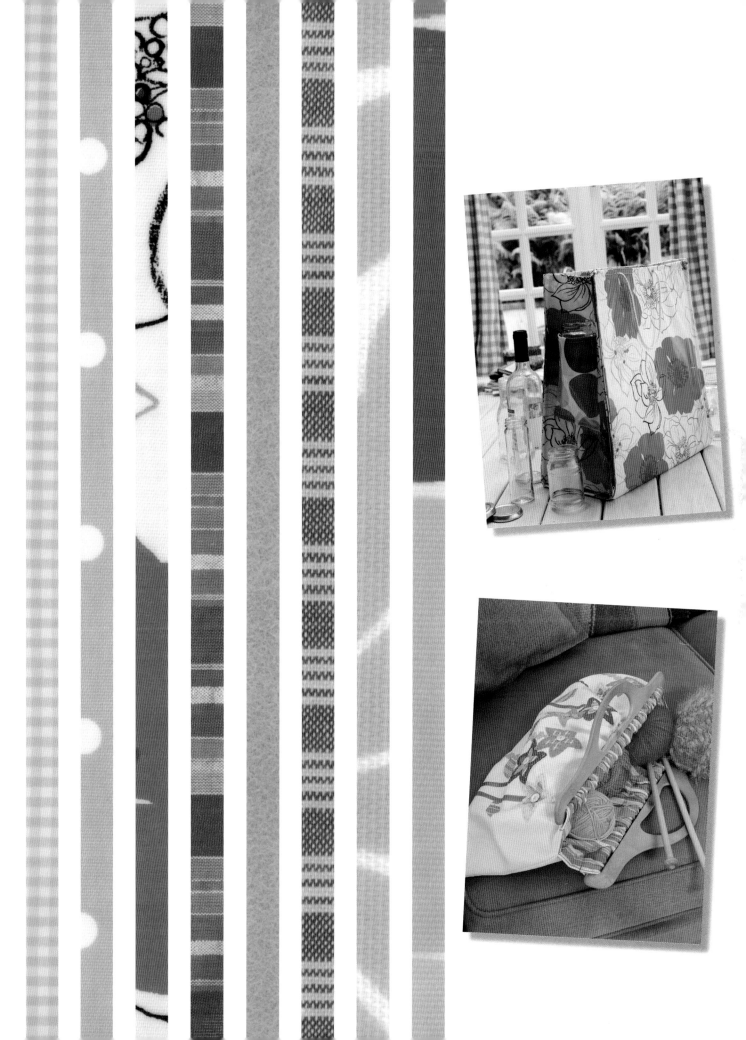

Wash day pinks

Put an end to wash day blues by making this oh-so-simple personalised drawstring bag to keep your laundry out of sight. However, the sassy undies design means you'll definitely want to keep the bag on display, and everyone will want one. So with mini variations for the kids too (see page 76), there should be no reason why the whole family shouldn't keep their laundry neat and tidy!

LOVE THE LOOK?

If your clean clothes start feeling a little envious of those waiting in their lovely new laundry bag to be washed, why not make these dinky scented sachets for your wardrobe and drawers (see page 75).

fabulous fabric

The main body of the bags are made out of a heavy cream cotton fabric. This is paired with traditional pink-for-girls and blue-for-boys cotton fabrics in spots and gingham.

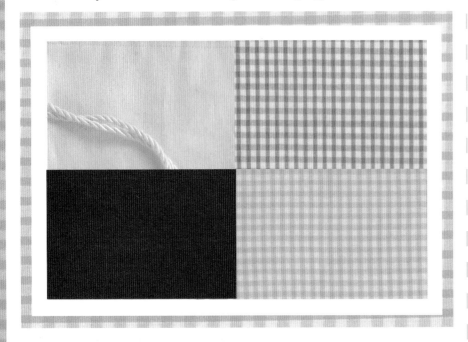

bag the essentials:

* Heavy cream cotton twill fabric
* Pink polka dot fabric
* Pink gingham fabric
* Pink floral fabric
* Deep pink lining fabric
* Cream sewing thread
* Pink machine embroidery thread
* Embroidery threads in pale pink, deep pink and lilac
* 2 yellow flower-shaped buttons
* Pink drawstring cord, 3m (120in)
* Safety pin
* Basic bag kit (see page 101)

finished size 120 x 50cm (48 x 20in)

1 Cut the cream twill fabric to 104 x 94 cm (41½ x 38in), and the pink polka dot fabric to 104 x 22 cm (41½ x 8⅝in).

2 Pin the two fabrics right side together along the long edge. Sew together, open the seam and then press with an iron.

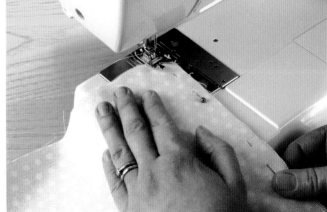

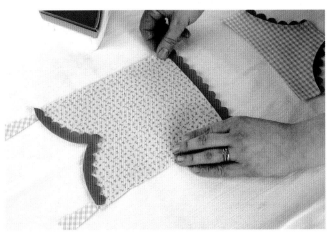

3 Use the pattern on page 123 to trace the shapes of the vest and pants onto bondaweb. Roughly cut out and iron onto the back of the chosen fabrics. Cut out.

4 Position the pieces onto the front of the cream fabric, peel off the paper backing and iron to fix in place. Make sure you leave a gap in between the bottom of the vest and the top of the briefs for the writing.

ARM CANDY
Instead of writing your name on the bag, you could label it 'laundry'. Or if you're super organised, make up three bags labelled 'dark', 'white' and 'coloured', choosing fabrics for the appliqué accordingly.

5 Write your chosen word in large letters between the vest and pants using a vanishing fabric marker pen. Use a darning foot on your sewing machine and drop the feed dog so you can sew around the letters freehand.

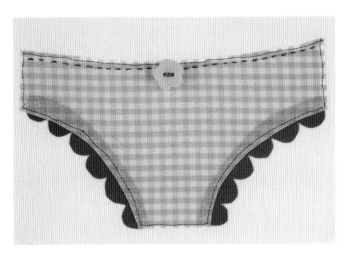

6 Machine stitch the vest and pants down securely using pink machine embroidery thread. Sew a button onto the vest and pants in the centre top. Sew running stitch in pale pink thread along the top edge off the vest. Use deep pink thread to sew running stitch along the bottom edge of the vest and the top of the pants

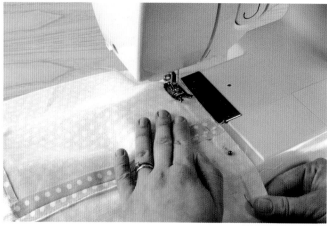

7 Use deep pink thread to sew a line of running stitch along the bottom of the cream fabric just above the seam with the pink polka dot fabric.

8 Fold the fabric in half, right sides together and pin the edges together to make the back seam. Sew with cream thread then open and press the seam flat. Position that seam so that it's in the centre back of the bag (still inside out) and pin the bottom of the bag. Machine stitch.

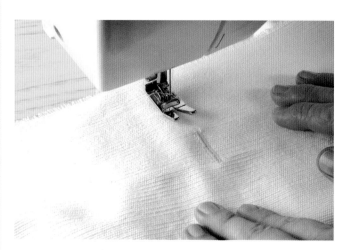

9 At either side of the bag, measure 32cm (12⅔in) down from the top and make a mark. Sew a buttonhole 3cm (1⅛in) long from this point on each side. Fold the top of the bag inside by 25cm (9⅞in) and press with the iron. Pin from buttonhole to buttonhole and then sew top and bottom to make a channel to run the drawstring through.

10 Cut the drawstring cord so that you have two pieces, each 150cm (60in). Thread them through at either side using a safety pin. Tie the ends together. Sew a line of running stitch in lilac around the top edge of the laundry bag.

Heaven scent

These little scented sachets only need a few scraps of fabric, but make gorgeous last-minute gifts. Like the laundry bag, why not personalise them with a name?

bag the essentials:

❀ Gingham fabric, blue or pink
❀ White cotton fabric
❀ Lining fabric, blue or pink
❀ Embroidery threads in pale blue or deep pink
❀ 2 ribbons, 30cm (12in) in length, blue or pink
❀ Cream machine thread
❀ Cotton wool/soft toy wadding and essential oil, or dried lavender
❀ Basic bag kit (see page 101)

finished size 11 x 7cm (4³⁄₈ x 2³⁄₄in)

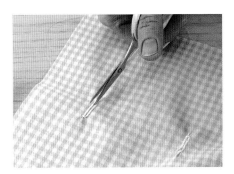

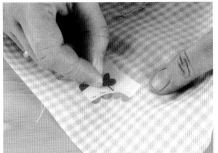

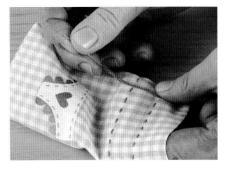

1 Firstly cut the gingham fabric to measure 18cm (7in) square. Then make two buttonholes, each 7cm (2³⁄₄in) down from the top of the fabric and 5cm (2in) in from the edge. The buttonholes should measure 1.5cm (⁵⁄₈in) in length.

2 Trace your chosen shapes from the patterns provided (see page 122) onto bondaweb and iron onto the back of the appropriate fabrics. Cut out. Iron these shapes onto the gingham fabric in the centre, 2 or 3cm (³⁄₄ or 1¹⁄₈in) up from the bottom edge. Add stitching to embellish.

3 Fold the gingham fabric in half, right sides together to make the back seam. Pin and sew. Open the hem and press with an iron. Place the seam to the centre back of the bag and pin and sew the bottom hem. Fold in the top edge by 5cm (2in) and press. Sew running stitch around the bag at the top and bottom of the buttonholes to make the channel for the drawstring. Thread the two lengths of ribbon through the channel tie the ends. Fill the bags with dried lavender or scented cotton wool.

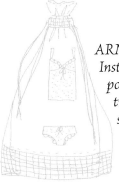

ARM CANDY
Instead of filling the sachets with pot pourri or dried lavender, why not try putting scented soaps into the sachets instead?

boys and girls

These smaller versions are well worth the effort if you're on a mission to make your little terror tidy up after themselves. The bold patterns and bright colours are particularly attractive to children, so fingers crossed…

The basic design

Cut the cream twill fabric to 84 x 72cm (32 x 28⅝in) and the contrasting bottom fabric to 84 x 16cm (32 x 6¼in). Make the bags in the same way as described for the adult's laundry bag. Make the buttonholes 12cm (4¾in) down from the top of the bags at each side, and fold the top in by 20cm (8in).

BLUE FOR YOU

Make the vest and pants from polka dot fabric with lining fabric for the edges. Embellish these with running stitch at the top of the vest in pale blue thread, and at the bottom of the vest in mid blue thread. Sew pale blue running stitch at the top of the pants too. Stitch two tiny buttons onto the vest at the right hand shoulder. Sew a line of running stitch at the bottom of the bag above the gingham strip in mid blue thread, and at the top edge of the bag in pale blue thread.

ARM CANDY
Choose funky co-ordinating patches to go in the middle of the bags. These can be made easily from complementary fabrics and colours. Or look out for the huge variety of ready made patches available.

bag the essentials:

*(boy's **or** girl's bag)*

- ❀ *Heavy blue **or** pink gingham fabric*
- ❀ *Blue **or** pink polka dot fabric*
- ❀ *Blue **or** lilac lining fabric*
- ❀ *2 tiny pale blue **or** pink flower shaped buttons*
- ❀ *Embroidery thread, pale blue, mid blue **or** pale pink, lilac, deep pink*
- ❀ *Machine embroidery thread, mid blue **or** purple*
- ❀ *White drawstring cord, 2 x 150 cm*
- ❀ *Basic bag kit (see page 101)*

finished size: 84 x 72cm (32 x 28⅝in)

PRETTY IN PINK

Make the vest and pants from polka dot fabric with lining fabric for the edges. Embellish these with running stitch at the top and bottom of the vest in lilac thread, and at the top of the pants in pale pink. Sew a button onto the vest and pants with pale pink thread. Sew running stitch at the bottom of the bag above the gingham strip in lilac thread and at the top edge of the bag in deep pink thread.

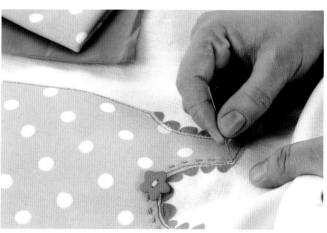

Ladies' day

This is the ideal toiletry bag for travelling – it's compact, waterproof and when you get there you simply unfold it and hang it up, and all your essentials are stored neatly. Not to mention the appeal of its boudoir-chic style, with luxurious lace and velvet trim! All you need to go with it is some sexy undies, a great outfit and the matching make-up bag on page 84 to create utter head-to-toe gorgeousness!

LOVE THE LOOK?

Pink and black is an irresistibly sexy combination. Continue the theme with a matching sassy make-up bag (see page 84) to ensure you look fabulous day and night!

fabulous fabric

The fabric used in this project is PVC coated so that it's wipe clean. This is most commonly used for table coverings so look in the furnishing department to find it.

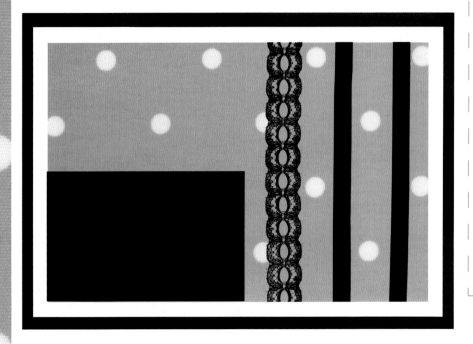

bag the essentials:

- ❋ Pink polka dot PVC fabric
- ❋ Black satin lining fabric
- ❋ Black lace ribbon
- ❋ Black satin ribbon, 1cm (½in) width
- ❋ Black velvet ribbon, 1cm (½in) width
- ❋ Pale pink embroidery thread
- ❋ Glass button
- ❋ Black and pale pink sewing thread
- ❋ Basic bag kit (see page 101)

finished size (unrolled)
43 x 17.5cm (17 x 6⅘in)

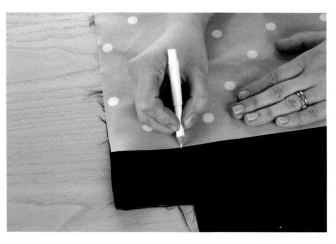

1 Use a pencil to mark out the size of the pink fabric on the reverse. You need a piece 20 x 47cm (7⁹⁄₁₀ x 18.5⁵⁄₁₀in). Cut out.

2 Use this piece as a template to draw around so you can cut the same size out of the black lining fabric.

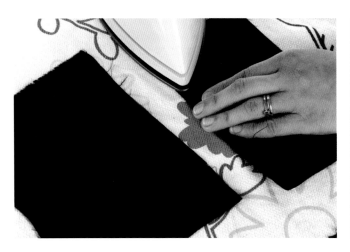

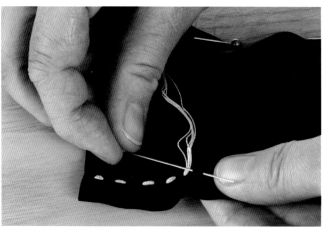

3 Cut three pieces of black lining fabric, each 11 x 18cm (4³⁄₁₀ x 7in) for pockets. Fold over the top edge twice, press with an iron, pin and sew.

4 Sew running stitch in pale pink embroidery thread along the top edge of all three pockets.

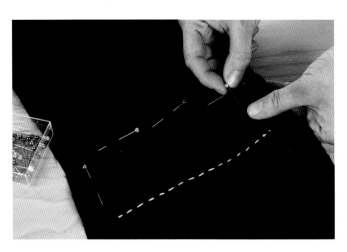

5 Use a fabric pencil to mark the fold points onto the lining. Measuring from the top edge, you need a line at 16.5cm (6½in) down, and another at 31.5cm (12²⁄₅in) down. Fold and press the side and bottom edges on each pocket and then pin them in place onto the large piece of black fabric.

6 Sew them in place. Then mark, pin and sew the top and bottom pockets in half.

7 Place the lining and the pink fabrics together, right sides facing. Pin around the edges and sew, leaving the top edge open.

8 Snip the corners diagonally and then turn through to the right side. Press lightly with an iron to flatten, taking care to protect the pink fabric from direct heat so it doesn't melt.

9 Fold the raw edges of the opening inwards and pin. Make a loop out of a 16cm (6³⁄₁₀in) length of black satin ribbon and pin this into the opening in the middle. Stitch the opening closed.

10 Pin on the velvet ribbon and the black lace near the top edge and sew in place.

11 Next, pin and sew along the fold points, as shown in the photograph.

12 Sew on the glass button so that the loop will fit over it when the toiletry bag is rolled up.

CHILD'S PLAY

Kids don't have to be left out in the smart washbag stakes. Make bathtime fun with this playful toiletries bag. This is made in the same way as the make-up bag, but is slightly larger. When you make the paper template, the top edge should be 21cm (8⁵⁄₁₀in), the bottom edge 28cm (11in) and the depth 19cm (7½in). A sophisticated adult's version can be made following the instructions on page 84.

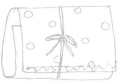

ARM CANDY
Buy small travel sized items to fit into this bag, and decant shampoos and shower gels into smaller bottles.

Lipstick chick

This make-up bag is the perfect companion to the toiletry bag. Keep all your favourite cosmetics safe in this neat little zipped bag, with velvet and lace to add a touch of luxury and decadence!

bag the essentials:

❄ Pink polka dot PVC-coated fabric
❄ Black velvet ribbon, 1cm (½in) width
❄ Black lace ribbon
❄ Black satin ribbon, 1cm (½in) width
❄ Pink zip, 16cm (6³⁄₁₀in) length
❄ Cream machine thread
❄ Basic bag kit (see page 101)

finished size 21 x 12cm (8⁵⁄₁₀ x 4⁷⁄₁₀in)

1 Make a paper template with the top edge 18cm (7in) long, the bottom edge 24cm (9²⁄₅in) and the depth 14cm (5½in). Use this template to mark out and cut two pieces of the pink waterproof fabric.

2 Fold over the top edge of each piece by 1cm (½in) and pin onto either side of a 16cm (6³⁄₁₀in) pink zip. Sew in place.

ARM CANDY
You can use this template to make a matching purse. Use a heavier cotton fabric, and decorate with beads and sequins as well as ribbons.

3 Pin a length of black velvet ribbon and black lace onto the front panel near the top and sew.

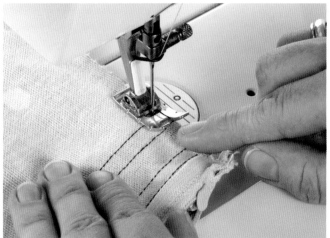

4 Fold the bag so it looks inside out. Open the zip and pin the sides and bottom edge. Sew and snip the corners. Turn through to the right side. Finish by attaching a 20cm (7⁹⁄₁₀in) length of black satin ribbon to the zip pull.

Going green

Do your bit for the planet and store all your things to be recycled in this amazing bag. As it's so solid it can stand like a box in your cupboard. It's made from PVC-coated fabric so it's wipe clean, it is roomy enough to fit loads of stuff in, and it's stylish too! When it's empty the base is removable so it can be stored flat. So whether you keep your old newspapers, bottles or jars in it, it will brighten your kitchen and make recycling a pleasure!

LOVE THE LOOK?

Becoming an eco-warrior and keeping old magazines for recycling doesn't mean you can't be stylish too. This groovy magazine file will look at home in any living room, bathroom or bedroom, see page 90.

fabulous fabric

Again, the fabric is PVC coated. This makes the bag strong and easy to clean. It's made from two different prints, which are linked by common colours to make them sit well together.

bag the essentials:

❈ PVC-coated fabric in floral print and spotted print
❈ Eyelet punch and eyelets
❈ Plastic stiffener
❈ Cream cord
❈ Cream sewing thread
❈ Basic bag kit (see page 101)

finished size 49 x 36cm (19³⁄₁₀ x 14⁷⁄₁₀in)

ARM CANDY
Make this bag in green coloured fabrics and use it to keep all your gardening bits and bobs safe and tidy.

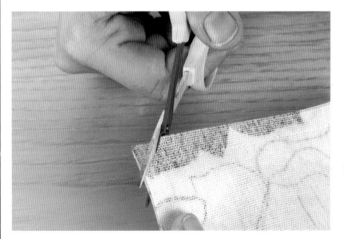

1 Cut the floral PVC-coated fabric so that you have one piece 99 x 38cm (38 x 15in) and two pieces 47 x 38cm (18½ x 15in). Lie the large piece face up and place the two smaller pieces on top of it, right sides facing, so that one piece fits at the top of the large piece and one at the bottom, with a gap in between in the middle. Pin these pieces in place and sew. Snip the corners diagonally and turn through to the right side, so it makes two pockets.

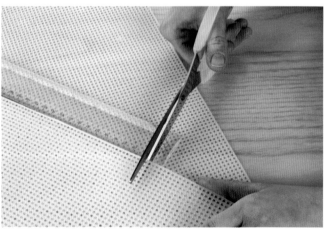

2 Cut the plastic stiffener so that you have two pieces, each 34 x 38.5cm (13 x 15in) and then slide them into the two pockets.

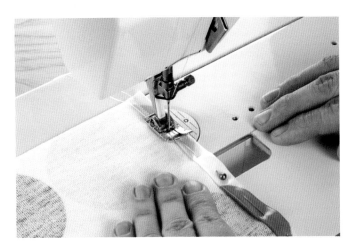

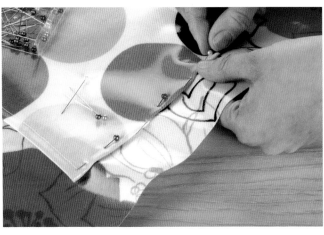

3 Cut four more pieces of the floral fabric for the sides of the bag, two pieces 21 x 40cm (8½ x 16in) and two pieces 21 x 43cm (8½ x 17in). Cut two pieces of spotted fabric for pockets, each 20 x 15cm (7⁹⁄₁₀ x 6in). Double fold the top edge of each pocket, pin and stitch.

4 Fold the side and bottom edges in by 1cm (½in) and then pin onto the longer of the two side panels 15cm (7⁹⁄₁₀in) from the top. Stitch the pockets in place.

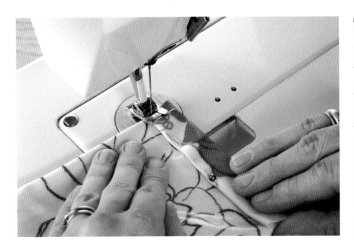

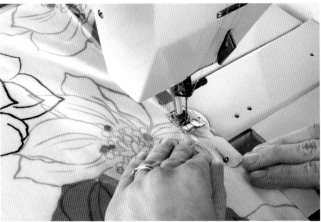

5 Place the two side pieces together, right sides facing so that one piece is longer than the other. Pin and sew together, leaving the bottom open. Snip the corners diagonally and turn through to the right side. Double fold the flap at the bottom so that it makes a hem on the inside of the side panel and sew.

6 Pin the side panels in place on the main panel of the bag, so that the side panels are flush with the top edges of the bag. Sew in position.

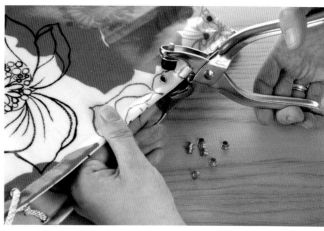

7 Cut the plastic stiffener so you have a piece 17 x 34cm (6.5 x 13.5in). Cover this piece with spotted fabric, using double-sided tape to hold it securely in place. Push it into position at the bottom of the bag.

8 Use an eyelet punch to make holes at the top of the bag, so that the cord can be threaded through to make two handles.

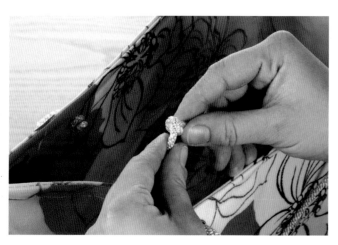

9 Cut two lengths of cream cord, each piece 60cm (24in). Thread them through the holes and secure by tying a knot at the ends of the cord.

ARM CANDY
Why not make several of these files to keep all your paperwork neat and tidy and easy to find?

SINGLE FILE

Keep magazines in this funky holder until they are ready for the recycling bag. The plastic coated fabric is ideal to cover boxes and files as it's easy to cut to size and the edges won't fray. Using spray adhesives gives much better control when sticking it onto the file, as it can be repositioned if needs be, before the glue dries to ensure a perfect finish. Simply cover a wooden magazine file with green floral print PVC fabric using spray adhesive. Stick the side panels first, then the front and back panels.

Arts and flowers

Although this bag is big and contains enough pockets to store all your craft bits and bobs, from knitting needles to fabric scraps, beads to embroidery threads, you might find it just too pretty to keep indoors! Sturdy yet beautiful, it is ideal for storing items from all hobbies and pastimes.

LOVE THE LOOK?

All that crafting is hard work so rest your head on this stunning cushion. Too good to waste in your workroom, why not make a set for the living room. Using the same techniques as the hobby bag, discover how to make it on page 98.

fabulous fabric

The body of the bag is made from a very heavy cream cotton fabric which gives the bag a sturdiness. The lining, by contrast is a fine cotton print in shades of pink, orange and red. This colour palette is repeated in the appliqué flowers in felt and again with the ribbons and braid.

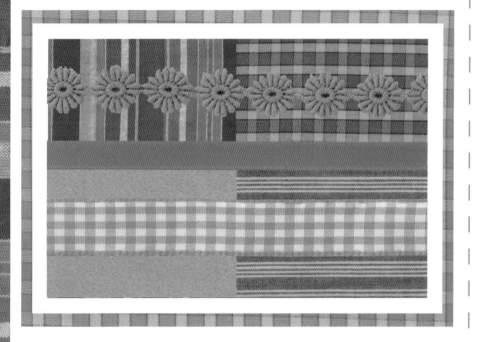

1 Cut two pieces of heavy cream fabric, each 28 x 52cm (11 x 20½in). Cut one piece of striped cotton fabric 56 x 52cm (22 x 20½in). Trace seven large flower shapes, seven small flower shapes and seven leaf shapes (see page 124) onto bondaweb. Iron the large flower shapes onto various colours of felt. Iron the smaller flowers and leaves onto the patterned fabrics. Cut out all the shapes.

2 Arrange the felt flowers onto the front piece of the bag (cream fabric) and mark where you want the stems to be. Cut lengths of the various ribbons and use fabric glue to stick them in position. Allow to dry.

bag the essentials:

❀ Heavy cream furnishing fabric
❀ Striped cotton fabric in pinks, oranges and red
❀ Scraps of patterned cotton fabrics in similar colours
❀ Felt, shades of pink and orange
❀ Selection of braids and ribbons in pinks and orange
❀ Embroidery thread in pinks and orange
❀ Long wooden handles
❀ Sewing machine thread in cream and pink
❀ 7 cream buttons
❀ Basic bag kit (see page 101)

finished size 45 x 30cm (17⁷⁄₁₀ x 12in)

3 Iron the felt flowers in place at the ends of the stems and iron the smaller flowers inside the felt flowers. Arrange the leaves onto the stems and iron to fix in place. Sew running stitch around the edge of the felt flowers with embroidery thread, and also along the centre of the leaves. Sew buttons in the centre of all the flowers.

4 Mark the two cream panels that will form the front and back of the bag at points 10cm (4in) down from the top edge on each side. Place these two pieces face to face and pin and sew around the sides and bottom from mark to mark. Snip the corners diagonally and turn through to the right side.

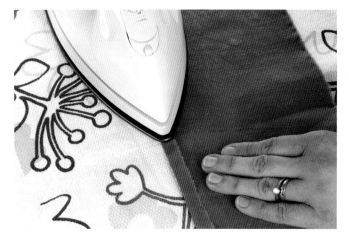

5 Cut two pieces of striped fabric, each 32 x 15cm (13 x 6in). These will be pockets inside the bag. Double fold, pin and sew the top (long) edge of each. Fold under the sides and bottom edge by 1cm (½in) and press.

6 Take the large piece of striped fabric and fold in half, so that the width is still 52cm (20½in). Pin the pockets onto this fabric, each pocket 5cm (2in) up from the centre fold. Sew along the sides and bottom. Mark each pocket into three sections and sew along these marks.

7 Fold the lining panel in half, pockets inside, and mark each side 10cm (4in) down from the top edge. Pin down the sides and stitch from mark to mark. Place the lining inside the bag. At each side, fold the raw edges inside and stitch, so that the lining and outside of the bag are stitched together along the 10cm (4in) split at either side.

8 Next, tack the lining to the bag along the top edges, as shown in the photograph.

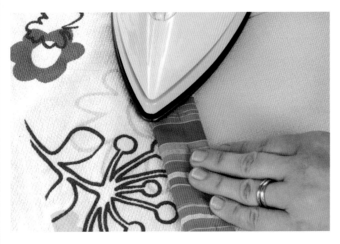

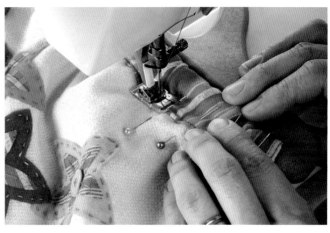

9 Fold the top edge of the bag over by 1cm (½in) to hide raw edges. Fold it again so that the lining is folded onto the front of the bag by 3cm (1⅕in) and press with the iron.

10 Push this fabric through the handles, pin and sew. Remove tacking.

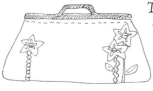

ARM CANDY
Try making this bag in a vintage look 'carpet bag' style by using heavy embroidered furnishing fabrics in darker colours. Omit the appliqué embellishments.

INSIDE OUT
Choose an attractive inner lining which will catch the eye when the bag falls open and all your craft materials are on show (opposite). Use the inner pockets of this bag to keep smaller items such as needles, pins, beads and buttons safe and easy to find.

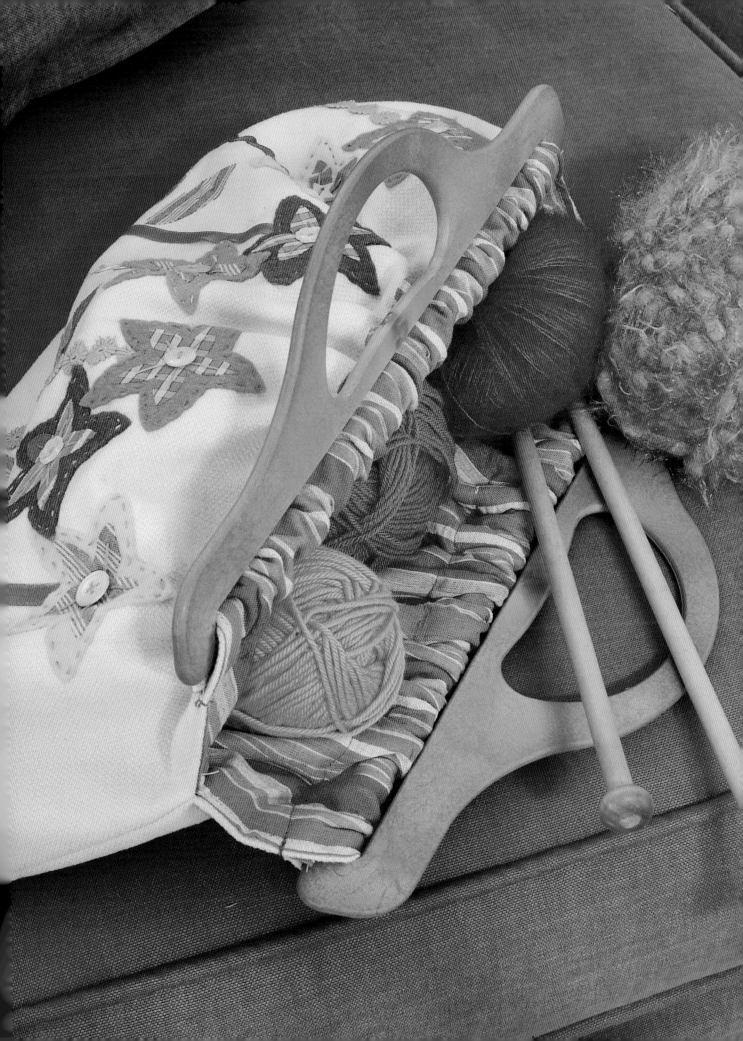

Pillow talk

Cushions with envelope backs are extremely easy to make as there's no need for buttons or zips. You can really go to town and be creative with the stitching, ribbons and braids to create a fabulous and detailed handcrafted cushion.

1 Take a cushion pad 26 x 36cm (10 x 13.5in). Cut cream fabric so you have one piece 28 x 38cm (11 x 15in), and two pieces 28 x 25cm (11 x 9½in). Trace three large flowers, three small flowers and five leaves (see page 124) onto bondaweb. Iron the large flowers onto felt, and the small flowers and leaves onto patterned fabric. Cut out all the shapes.

2 The large cream fabric will be the cushion front. Arrange various ribbons onto this panel in stripes, and arrange flowers (the smaller flowers ironed onto the larger flowers) and leaves. When happy, mark the positions with a fabric pen. Use fabric glue to stick the ribbons in place. When dry iron the flowers and leaves to fix. Decorate this panel with hand stitching in embroidery threads.

3 The two smaller cream panels will form the back of the cushion. Double fold and hem one of the 28cm (11in) edges on each panel.

4 Place the front of the cushion face up and pin the back panels so that the raw edges match the raw edges of the front panel and they overlap in the middle to form an 'envelope'. Stitch the cover together and snip corners diagonally. Turn to right side and iron. Push cushion pad into the cover at the opening at the back.

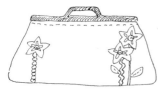

ARM CANDY
Simply adjust the sizes to fit any cushion pad you have – you could even make a tiny one and use it as a pin cushion!

Techniques
Getting Started

Before you start, there are several items needed to make the bags in this book. Not all of them are essential but most will be used at some point or other. The items listed here are all easy to find and cheap to buy, with the exception of a sewing machine perhaps. Make sure you have plenty of needles (both hand sewing and machine) before you start as it's very easy to lose or break them.

Basic Sewing Kit

The Basic Bag Kit that you will need for the projects in this book includes most, if not all, of the basic sewing kit below. Gather these materials before you start so that they are handy while you are making the bags.

TOP TIP
It's worth investing in good quality dressmaking scissors as they will give a clean cut to your fabric.

1 Iron
You will need an iron and an ironing surface for bag assembly after each stage of construction.

2 Fabric markers
Vanishing markers are ideal, as they disappear after several hours on their own, or with a little water, so won't leave a mark once the sewing is completed

3 Fabric pencils
Use fabric pencils or tailors' chalk to draw a line or pattern. The pencil marks simply rub off once the stitching is complete.

4 Pins
Use pins when assembling bags to keep the pieces together before finally sewing.

5 Ruler
You will need a ruler for measuring or marking out the lines for then cutting against.

6 Tape measure
A good quality tape measure is handy for measuring long lengths where a ruler is too short.

7 Bondaweb
This comes in a roll or in pre-cut pieces and looks like paper. One side can be drawn on and the other has a thin membrane of glue which melts when heated by an iron to stitch the two fabrics together.

8 Fabric glue
Fabric glue is essential for attaching ribbons, braids and lengths of sequins, where you don't want to see stitching.

9 Double-sided tape
Although not an essential piece of kit, this will come in handy when you want to fix items temporarily.

10 Dressmaking and embroidery scissors
Embroidery scissors are useful as they have small sharp blades, ideal for cutting thread. Use dressmaking scissors for cutting fabric.

11 Needles
Hand, beading and machine needles are available in many sizes and for many purposes. When sewing, choose a needle that matches the thickness of the thread you are using, so the thread passes easily through the fabric. Use an appropriate machine needle for your work and change it frequently – immediately if damaged or bent.

12 Sewing and embroidery threads
You will need good quality cotton thread for sewing patchwork and for bag assembly. These are easy to cut and sew and don't fray too readily. It is essential to use a strong thread when attaching beads to bags so they do not come adrift. Embroidery threads are thicker threads than sewing, suitable for embroidered embellishments.

Other Essentials

Sewing machine
A sewing machine will produce much stronger seams than hand sewing, and is a lot quicker and easier. If you haven't got access to a sewing machine just make smaller bags that won't be required to contain heavy loads.

Lining fabric

Linings make the inside of your bag look a lot neater, and allows you to use even more fantastic fabrics. You can choose thin and silky lining fabrics that match the colours of your bag, or use cotton fabrics that are brightly coloured to contrast with the fabric of your bag.

Preparation

Before you do any sewing it pays to spend a little time making sure the material is ready. By ensuring you have all the tools and items needed to make the bags you won't need to leave the project at a delicate stage to hunt for something to hold it together with!

Pinning

This may seem very basic, but if you pin fabric correctly before sewing then it can make it a lot easier to stitch!

Pinning Edges and Hems

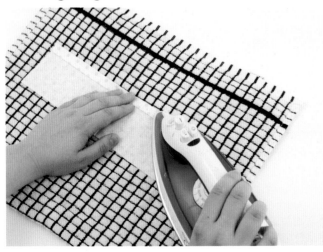

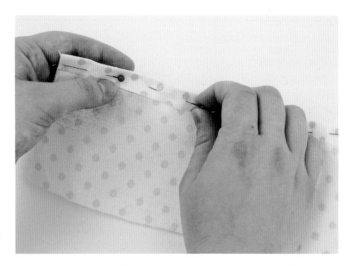

1 Fold the edge of the fabric over and press with an iron. Fold a second time to hide any raw edges and then press again.

2 Place the pins along the edge so that the end of the pin is at the right-hand side. This means that you can pull the pins out easily as you stitch.

Pinning Fabrics Together

When pinning two fabrics together you can use the basic technique above, or this one, which delivers better results, especially if the fabrics are slippery or stretchy (*).

1 Place the fabrics together, edge to edge. Pin at right angles to the edge to the fabrics, leaving a small gap between the pins.

TOP TIP
When you stitch on a sewing machine you can sew straight over the pins, if they are pinned at right angles to the line of stitching (go fairly slowly), and remove them at the end.

Tacking

Tacking fabrics together is a very quick and easy way of making sure that they stay in place as you sew them. As the stitches are removed at the end you needn't worry about them being neat. It also helps if you use a contrasting coloured thread to the fabric you're stitching, as this makes the stitches stand out so that they are easier to see when you come to unpick them.

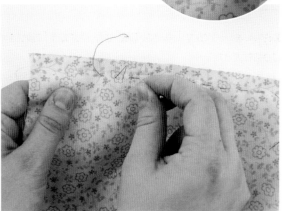

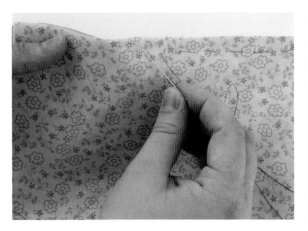

1 Using a thin thread sew the fabrics together using large running stitches, without a knot at the end of the fabric.

2 Once the fabrics have been sewn together with a sewing machine, use a 'quick-unpick' tool or a pin to pull out the tacking stitches.

Marking Fabrics

It sometimes helps to mark out designs onto your fabrics before stitching so you can be sure to get it the way you want it (e.g. for the butterflies' antennae on the sunny afternoon project, page 42).

TOP TIP
As a general rule, vanishing pens are best for very detailed work, and for lighter coloured fabrics, and the pencil or chalk for darker coloured fabrics.

1 There are two ways of marking fabrics. The first is to use a vanishing pen which will disappear either on its own or with a little water. Use the pen to draw the line you want to follow with stitching. Once stitched, dab with a little water on your finger to remove any traces of the pen.

2 The second way is to use a fabric pencil/tailors' chalk, which will just rub off. Draw the line or pattern with the pencil and take care not to rub it out as you stitch. Once the stitching is complete, rub the pencil marks to remove.

Decorative Stitches

All the hand stitching in this book is very simple and easy to do, and I've included step-by-step instructions on how to do all the stitches featured. Embroidery threads are made up from several thin strands of thread (usually six) put together to make one thicker thread. Sometimes you may find this thread too thick to work with, in which case you can split the thread by pulling it apart so that you have a two or three stranded thread to work with instead. This is particularly useful when stitching smaller and more fiddly pieces, for example the stitching around the birds on the bon voyage bag, page 50.

Running Stitch

This can be used to sew two pieces of fabric together (e.g. to sew the flower shape onto the purse in the shopaholic! bag project, page 56), along hems, and for decoration (e.g. the arts and flowers bag, page 92).

Stitching Tips

❀ If you're right-handed you'll find it a lot easier to sew from right to left, and vice versa if you are left-handed.

❀ It's also important to try and keep the tension even as you sew and not to pull the thread too tight or you'll end up with a gathered and very buckled-looking fabric.

❀ Don't worry too much about your stitches all being exactly the same size or too neat as a slight unevenness can add to the quirky look!

1 Start by tying a small knot at the end of your thread. Push the needle from the back of the fabric through to the front.

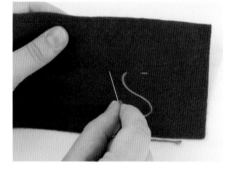

2 Make a small stitch and push the needle up again so that the gap between the stitches is about the same length as the actual stitches. Then begin your second stitch in the same way, as shown.

3 Pull the thread right through and then repeat.

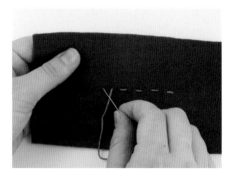

❀ *TOP TIP*
For running stitch, make the stitches on the underside equal length, but half the size or less than the upper stitches.

Laced Running Stitch

This stitch is used to make the tail of the birds in the bon voyage project, page 50.

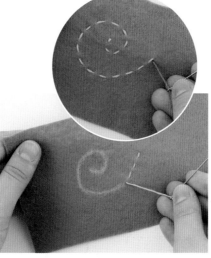

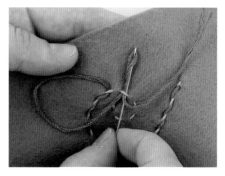

1 Mark out the lines that form the tail of the birds with a vanishing pen or fabric marker.

2 Sew running stitch, following the lines you have drawn. Using a different coloured thread, push the needle up halfway along the first stitch, just below it.

3 Use the wrong end of the needle to weave the thread through the running stitch from top to bottom.

Catch Stitch

I use this stitch to sew one piece of fabric to another when using appliqué, which works effectively on the girl about town bag and for the notebook, page 22.

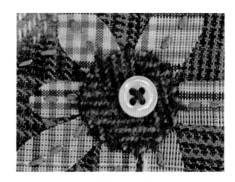

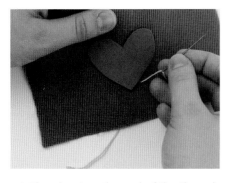

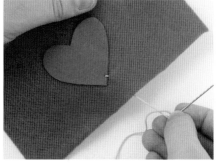

1 Tie a knot at the end of the thread and push up from the back of the fabric to the front, near the join of the two fabrics.

2 Make a small stitch that overlaps the two fabrics in a straight line. Push the needle back through to the back of the fabric.

3 Push the needle back to the front of the fabric a little way along from the first stitch and repeat.

French Knots

Also known as French dots, knotted stitch, twisted knot stitch and wound stitch, these are really useful for making small raised dots, especially in the centre of flowers or to make eyes, as here. The weight of the thread will determine the size of the finished stitch.

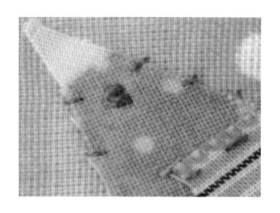

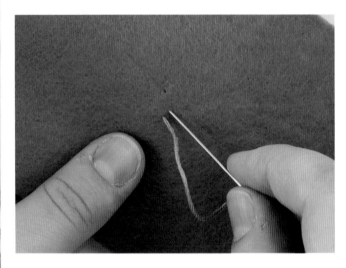

1 Tie a knot at the end of your thread. Bring the needle out from the back of the fabric at the point you wish to make the knot. Pull thread through completely. Push the needle back through right beside the entry point and make a tiny stitch with the point of the needle.

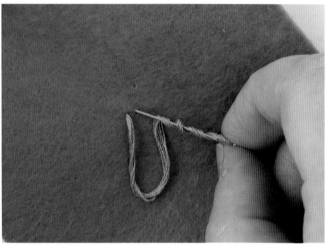

2 When the needle is only halfway out wrap the thread two or three times around the point of the needle.

3 Place your thumb firmly over the wrapped thread and pull the needle through.

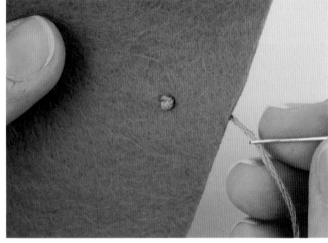

4 Push the needle back through the fabric right beside the knot and pull to finish the knot. Make a small stitch at the back of the fabric to tie off the thread.

Single Cross Stitch

This makes a nice decorative stitch, especially in patchwork or appliqué (e.g. the bon voyage bag, page 50).

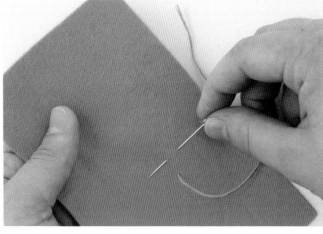

1 Push the needle up from the back of the fabric and pull the thread through completely. Place the needle back into the fabric at a diagonal downwards from the entrance point, and bring the needle point up in a straight line so that is on the same level as the entrance point.

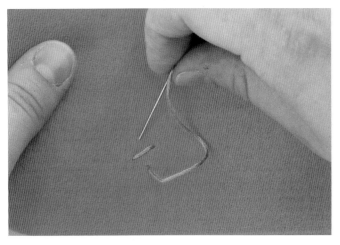

2 Pull the thread through so you have a diagonal stitch. Place the needle back into the fabric in a diagonal, so that it crosses over the first stitch and completes the 'x'.

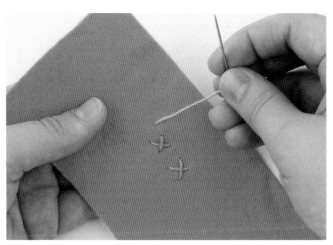

3 Repeat, making the next stitch a little way along from the first.

Fabric Glue

Fabric glue is ideal for attaching items that are too small or fiddly to stitch in place, or for ribbons and braid when you don't want to see any stitches (e.g. the sunny afternoon bag on page 42 or the arts and flowers bag on page 92). It's also very quick and easy to use!

1 Mark out where you want to glue on the ribbon or braid. Then apply a thin line of glue to both the fabric and the ribbon.

2 Press together and leave until completely dry (about 30 minutes). If there's any excess glue visible, remove when wet.

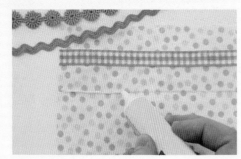

✳ TOP TIP
The glue can be made stronger by ironing gently over it when dry.

Easy Appliqué

Appliqué is the name for fabric shapes being stitched onto other fabrics. The easiest way to do this is using a product called bondaweb (or wonderweb, as it's sometimes known). This comes in a roll or in pre-cut pieces and looks like paper. One side can be drawn on (so you can trace the shape you want) and the other has a thin membrane of glue which melts when heated by an iron to stitch the two fabrics together. It's worth remembering that when you trace the designs you want onto bondaweb, they will come out in reverse. As the glue on the back of the bondaweb melts when heated, you have to be very careful to iron the paper side or else it will stick to your iron. If this does happen, use an iron cleaner (*) to remove it.

Tiny running stitches sewn around the edges of the cake add a touch of extra security and some decoration. When stitching on felt appliqué you will often get a slight quilted effect due to the thickness of the fabric which adds to the effect.

When using very thin and silky fabrics to appliqué with, the bondaweb will be sufficient to hold the pieces in place without any extra stitches. Check that the fabrics will not melt or burn when ironed beforehand.

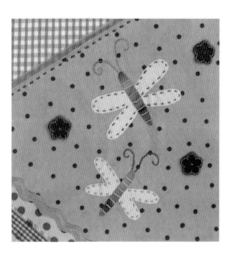

When using cotton fabrics to appliqué with, you will need extra stitching in addition to the bondaweb. Again, you can use this to provide decoration.

You can use a sewing machine to add the extra stitching to your appliqué after using thebondaweb – this will make it very secure. To sew freehand (i.e. not in straight lines) on the sewing machine you will need to use a darning foot and drop the feed dog so that the fabric moves freely.

1 Trace the shape you want onto the paper side of the bondaweb, as shown.

2 Cut roughly around this shape, and iron it onto the back of the fabric you wish to appliqué.

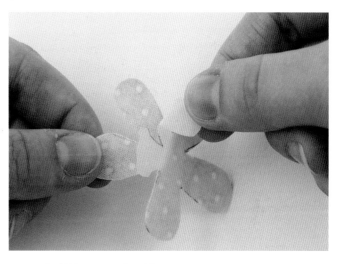

3 Then carefully cut out the shape, taking care to use smooth movements when cutting to prevent a jagged edge or line.

4 Peel off the paper backing.

5 Place the shape onto the backing fabric and iron to fix in position.

TOP TIP

When using bondaweb to attach fabrics together, always check that the fabric you use is able to be ironed without shrivelling or melting!

Simple Patchwork

There are two ways to get a patchwork effect used in this book. The first is using pieces of fabric backed with bondaweb and ironed onto a backing fabric (see Easy Appliqué, p108). The other way is to stitch individual pieces of fabric together (as used in the bon voyage bag on page 50).

Feature different prints for an interesting patchwork effect, as with the bon voyage case on page 50, which uses three fabrics in blue and white as the main colours. The floral patches add a hint of colour but the muted pastel shades give the case a vintage look.

Mix floral fabric with green spotted fabric for a retro feel, as with the shabby chic bag on page 10. The red gingham ribbon contributes to the patchwork theme. Both the main fabrics of the bag should be made out of the same fabric, such as cotton is used here.

Use a fresh and complementary blend of colours, like this pretty as a picture photo frame on page 48 which is made in using girly pink gingham with neutral dotty and floral fabrics accented with red stitching. A co-ordinating red fabric flower finishes off the look.

Create a detailed patchwork with stitched fabrics, motifs, ribbons and braids in vibrant toning shades of pink and orange, such as this pillow talk cushion on page 98. Complete the idea with felt flowers and cream buttons.

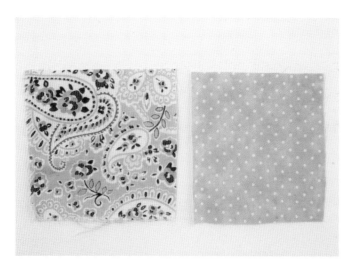

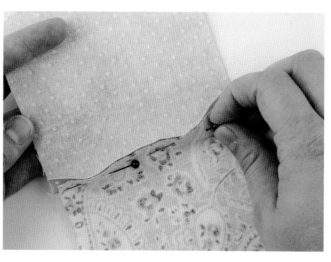

1 Cut pieces of the fabrics you want to use, making sure you add an extra 1cm (½in) all the way around to account for the hems.

2 Pin the pieces together, so that the right sides are facing each other.

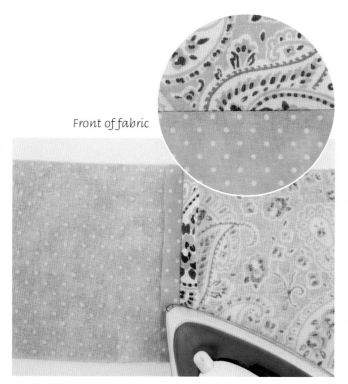

Front of fabric

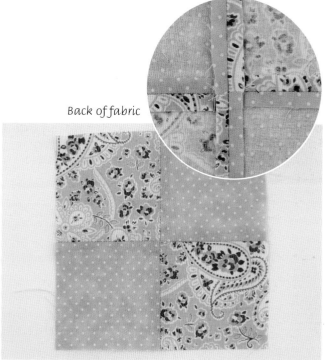

Back of fabric

3 Sew the two pieces together. Open the hem and press flat with an iron.

4 Build up the patchwork by adding more pieces of fabric, to finish.

✺ TOP TIP
When making patchwork you can either use all the same sized patches or vary them. It's easier if all the patches are square or rectangular shaped.

Quick Quilting

This is the technique used for the lace and ribbon quilted bag, page 16, in the shabby chic project on page 10. There are many different ways of quilting but this is one of the most basic and easiest. If you don't have a sewing machine then you can sew by hand, using tiny running stitches to provide the pattern. Always tack the fabrics together so that they won't move around as you quilt them.

Quilting your fabric gives the bag, such as this lace and ribbon bag on page 16, a fantastic tactile quality, and you can make it as basic or as complex as you choose.

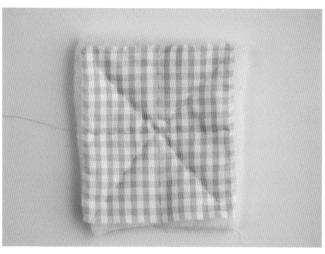

1 Cut three different fabrics to the same size – you need one fabric for the top layer, one fabric for the bottom layer and a layer of wadding in the middle.

2 Tack the three layers together, from top to bottom, side to side and corner to corner so you have a star shape tacked. You can also tack around the edges too.

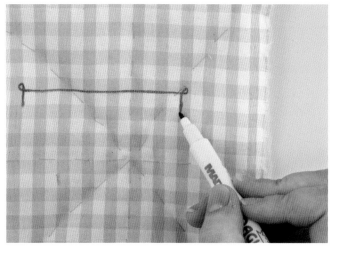

3 You can mark the design you want to sew with a vanishing pen or fabric pencil if you want, or just make a random design.

4 If using the sewing machine, drop the feed dog and use a darning foot to allow you to sew freehand. This will enable you to move the fabric around in any direction as you sew. If sewing by hand then it shouldn't be a problem as you will be free to sew in any direction anyway.

5 Grasp the fabric at the edges and sew, moving the fabric so that you control the stitching completely. When finished, unpick the tacking stitches.

Embellishments

Stitching on a few well-chosen embellishments can really glam up your bag, adding colour and style. You can probably find a button, bead, sequin or charm in any style or shape you care to imagine and they can provide the perfect finishing touches to make your bags ultra desirable. Make sure you arrange all the pieces onto your design before stitching so you can be sure of the best arrangement. It can also help to mark out where you want your embellishments with a fabric pencil or vanishing marker so that you know you are going to get the best finished look.

Beads

Beads look fantastic on a bag or garment, adding an elegant touch. If you're using tiny seed beads, make sure you have a very fine beading needle, as normal needles may not fit through the hole in the bead.

1 To stitch on a bead, simply thread your beading needle with fine thread, preferably in the same colour as the bead and tie a knot at the end. Push the needle through the fabric from back to front at the point you want the bead to be.

2 Thread the bead onto the needle and pull the thread through, then push the needle back through the same point it entered.

TOP TIP
Tip a small amount of beads out into the lid of a jar before you start to stop them from running all over your surface.

The charming denim flower chain keyring (page 38) uses several coloured wooden beads threaded onto pretty matching red ribbon as embellishment..

The green wooden bead sewn onto the front of the funky just in case mp3 player holder (page 33) is both pretty and practical as it is used to fasten the loop and also matches the pouch's colourway.

Buttons

Buttons can either be used as a practical fastening or as a fun embellishment to jazz up your designs. You can sew two- or four-holed buttons easily, either using two straight stitches or in a cross. Often it's good to mix two- and four-holed buttons together and stitch them on in different ways for a varied look.

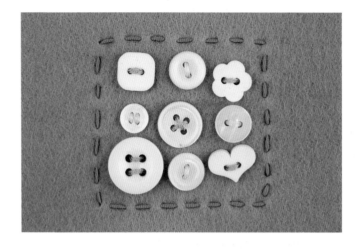

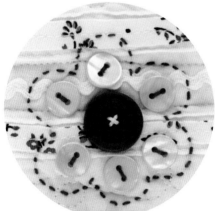

There are many different types of buttons available to add some extra pizzazz to your bag. Look for wooden, plastic, mother of pearl or more unusual types of buttons to decorate with.

TOP TIP
Take care choosing buttons to use, noting the shape, colour, and number of holes in the button (two or four).

Sequins

Sequins will always add a bit of sparkle to your design! You can stitch them on individually, but you will be able to see the thread, so make sure you sew carefully. Alternatively, you can sew them with a seed bead in the centre, which looks much neater. A seed bead sewn in the centre of a sequin will keep the sequin in place without any visable stitches.

Mark out where you want your sequins to be. A sequin in the middle of a motif, such as this floral flower, draws the eye to the embellishment (right).

TOP TIP
Always sew sequins concave side up.

Templates

All the templates you need for the bags are shown here. If you need to make a paper template, you can pin it onto the fabric and then either cut it out around the template or use a fabric pen or pencil to draw around the template and then cut it out. If you are cutting out multiple pieces the same size, it's often

quicker and easier to layer the fabrics and pin the template onto all of them so you can cut them out in one go. If you want to use the patterns at a smaller or larger size, simply photocopy the templates and enlarge or reduce as required.

TOP TIP
When tracing the shapes onto bondaweb, remember that the finished image will be reversed.

Bag outline

Glitz & Glamour (pages 64–67)

Note: This template is shown at 50%; you will need to enlarge by 200%.

Simply Dotty
(pages 18–19)

Evening Dress
(page 67)

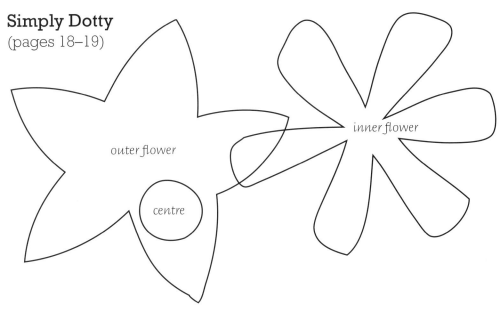

outer flower

inner flower

floral embellishment

centre

Lace and Ribbon
(pages 16–17)

Note: This template is shown at 50%;
you will need to enlarge by 200%.

bag outline

outer flower

Girl About Town
(pages 22–26)

inner
flower

flower
centre

flower
centre

inner
flower

top
flower
(outer)

I'll Check my Diary
(page 27)

Note: These templates are shown at 50% you will need to enlarge by 200%.

flower
centre

inner
flower

bottom
flower
(outer)

bottom flower

top flower

Funky Florals (pages 14–15)

Note: This template is shown at 50%; you will need to enlarge by 200%.

Sweet Treat (pages 20–21)

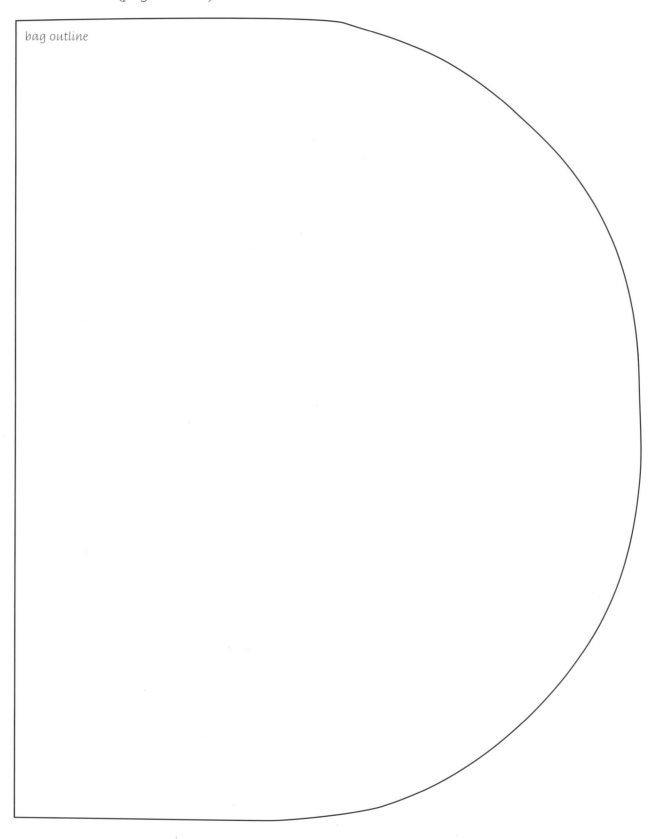

bag outline

Bon Voyage (pages 50–54)

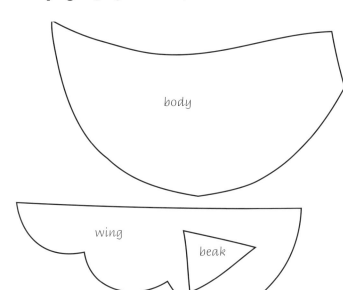

body

wing

beak

Magic Memories (page 55)

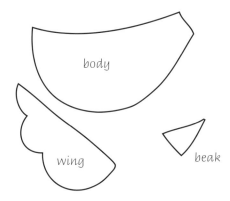

body

wing

beak

Sweet Treat (pages 20–21)

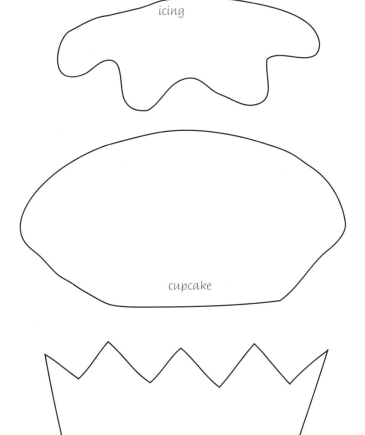

icing

cupcake

cupcake case

Boys and Girls (page 76)

Note: These templates are shown at 50%; you will need to enlarge by 200%.

arm
trim

Blue for You
vest

Pretty in Pink
vest

star motif

neck trim

heart motif

neck frill

top frill (girls)

pants
(boys & girls)

front trim (boys)

leg frills
(girls)

Wash Day Pinks
(pages 70–74)

Note: The templates on this page are shown at 50%; you will need to enlarge by 200%.

strap (cut two)

frills

Heaven Scent
(page 75)

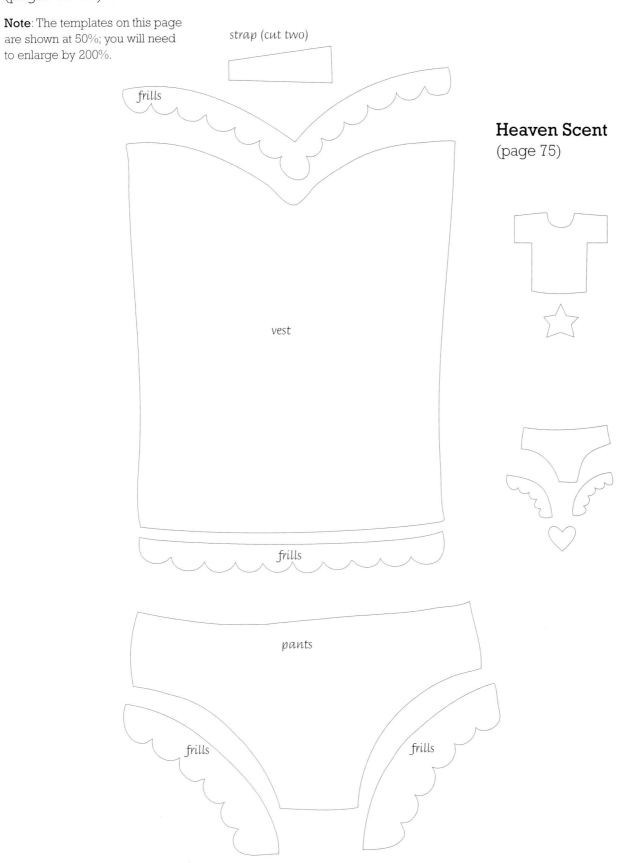

vest

frills

pants

frills

frills

Arts and Flowers (pages 92–97)

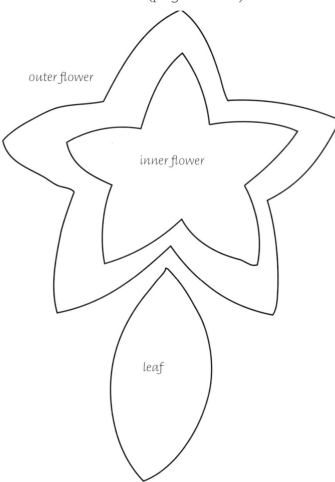

Shopaholic (pages 56–59)

Note: These templates are shown at 50%; you will need to enlarge by 200%.

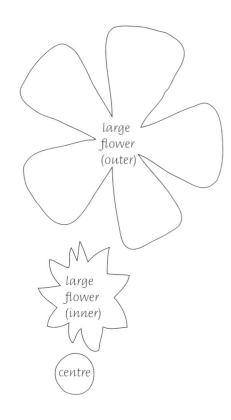

Pillow Talk (pages 98–99)

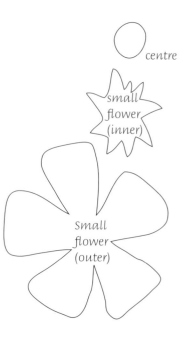

Pretty as a Picture
(page 48)

Sunny Afternoon
(pages 42–47)

Note: You will need to enlarge
by 450%

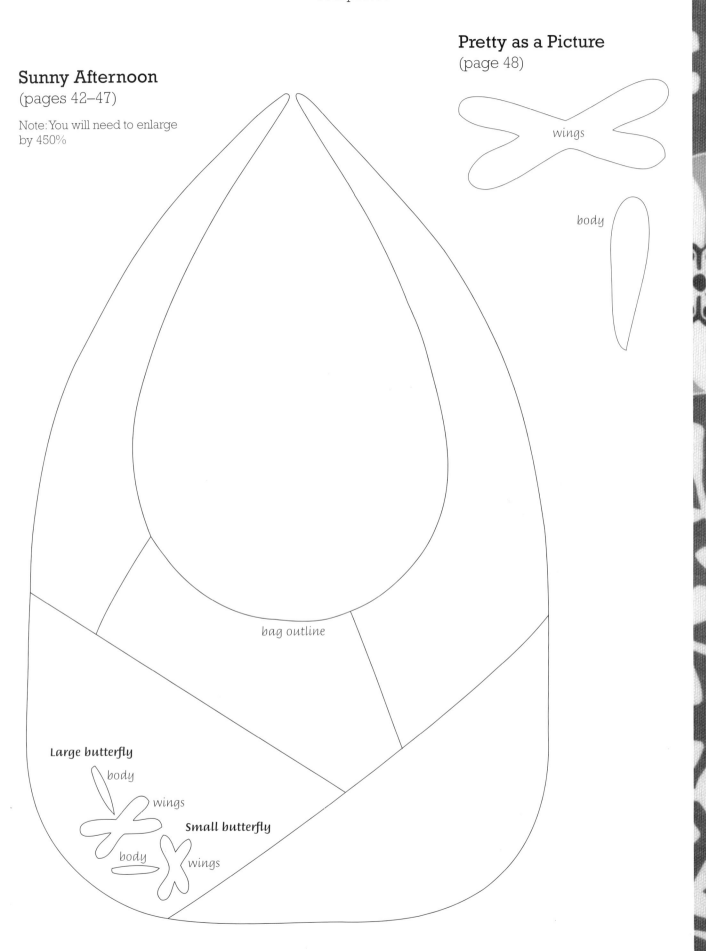

wings

body

bag outline

Large butterfly

body

wings

Small butterfly

body

wings

Suppliers

The following suppliers have a fantastic range of handles, fastenings, bottom studs, and clasps – in fact, all you need to turn your beautiful fabrics into fabulous bags!

UK

Bags Of Handles
22 Ascot Drive
Walton
Felixstowe
Suffolk IP11 9DW
Tel: 01394 279868
Email: sales@bagsofhandles.co.uk
Website: www.bagsofhandles.co.uk

The Bead Merchant
PO Box 5025
Coggleshall
Essex CO6 1HW
Tel: 01376 563567
Website: www.beadmerchant.co.uk

Craftynotions Ltd
Unit 2
Jessop Way
Newark NG24 2ER
Tel: 01636 700862
Website: www.craftynotions.com

Fun 2 Do
21 Scotch Street
Carlisle
Cumbria CA3 8PY
Tel: +44 (0)1228 523 843
Website: www.fun2do.co.uk

Gütermann Beads
For nearest stockist:
Perivale-Gütermann Ltd
Bullsbrook Road
Hayes
Middlesex UB4 OJR
Tel: 0208 589 1600

UK email:
perivale@guetermann.com
Europe email:
mail@guetermann.com

John Lewis
Nationwide chain of
department stores
Tel: 0845 604 9049 for stores and
website ordering details

JosyRose Ltd
PO Box 44204
London
E3 3XB
Tel: 0207 537 7755
Email: info@josyrose.com
Website: www.josyrose.com

U-Handbag
150 McLeod Road
London SE2 0BS
Tel: 0208 3103612
Email: info@u-handbag.com
Website: www.u-handbag.com

The Viking Loom
22 High Petergate
York Y01 7EH
Tel: +44 (0)1904 765599
Email:
vikingloom@vikingloom.co.uk
Website: www.vikingloom.co.uk

US

Bag Lady Press
PO Box 2409
Evergreen
CO 80437-2409
Tel: (303) 670 2177
Email: baglady@baglady.com
Website: www.baglady.com

Beadbox
1290 N. Scottsdale Road
Tempe Arizona 85281-1703
Tel: 1-800-232-3269
Website: www.beadbox.com

Distinctive Fabric
2023 Bay Street
Los Angeles
CA 90021
Tel: 877 721 7269
Website:
www.distinctivefabric.com

J&O Fabrics
9401 Rt.130
Pennsauken
NJ 08110
Tel: 856 663 2121
Website: www.jandofabrics.com

Gütermann of America Inc
8227 Arrowbridge Blvd
PO Box 7387
Charlotte
NC 28241-7387
Tel: (704) 525 7068
Email: info@gutermann-us.com

Acknowledgments

Many thanks to Maggie Allinson at Bags of Handles for her help, and also to my mum for her vast knowledge of all things stitch-y.

The publishers would like to thank Carlinos of Newton Abbot for accommodating the styled photography and Gillie James for the loan of her beautiful house and garden.

About the Author

Sally Southern is a textile artist and designer living and working in the seaside town of Cullercoats in the north east of England. She contributes regularly to craft magazines, is a community art worker, designs children's fashion and furnishing fabrics and produces her own work. She lives with her husband Stephen and young daughter Kitty (who, like her mum, also has an unhealthy interest in all things sparkly, button-like and beaded!). Sally has a lot of bags and never misses a chance to add to her collection.

Index